BACH: THE CELLO SUITES

Originally dismissed as curiosities, J. S. Bach's Cello Suites are now understood as the pinnacle of composition for unaccompanied cello. This handbook examines how and why Bach composed these highly innovative works. It explains the characteristics of each of the dance types used in the suites and reveals the compositional methods that achieve cohesion within each suite. The author discusses the four manuscript copies of Bach's lost original and the valuable evidence they contain on how the suites might be performed. He explores how, after around 1860, the Cello Suites gradually entered the concert hall, where they initially received a mixed critical and audience reception. The Catalan cellist Pablo Casals extensively popularized them through his concerts and recordings, setting the paradigm for several generations to follow. The Cello Suites now have a global resonance, influencing music from Benjamin Britten's Cello Suites to J-pop and media from K-drama to Ingmar Bergman's films.

EDWARD KLORMAN is Associate Professor and Canada Research Chair at the Department of Music Research, McGill University, having previously taught at The Juilliard School and Queens College, CUNY. His award-winning first book is *Mozart's Music of Friends: Social Interplay in the Chamber Works* (Cambridge, 2016).

NEW CAMBRIDGE MUSIC HANDBOOKS

Series Editor
NICOLE GRIMES, TRINITY COLLEGE DUBLIN

The New Cambridge Music Handbooks series provides accessible introductions to landmarks in music history, written by leading experts in their field. Encompassing a wide range of musical styles and genres, it embraces the music of hitherto under-represented creators as well as re-imagining works from the established canon. It will enrich the musical experience of students, scholars, listeners and performers alike.

Books in the Series

Hensel: String Quartet in E flat
Benedict Taylor

Berlioz: *Symphonie Fantastique*
Julian Rushton

Margaret Bonds: The *Montgomery Variations* and Du Bois *Credo*
John Michael Cooper

Robert Schumann: Piano Concerto
Julian Horton

Schoenberg: 'Night Music' – *Verklärte Nacht* and *Erwartung*
Arnold Whittall

Bach: The Cello Suites
Edward Klorman

Forthcoming Titles

Schubert: The 'Great' Symphony in C major
Suzannah Clark

Clara Schumann: Piano Concerto in A minor Op. 7
Julie Pedneault-Deslauriers

Donizetti: *Lucia di Lammermoor*
Mark Pottinger

Beethoven: String Quartet Op. 130
Elaine Sisman

Louise Farrenc: Nonet for Winds and Strings
Marie Sumner Lott

Cavalleria rusticana and *Pagliacci*
Alexandra Wilson

BACH: THE CELLO SUITES

EDWARD KLORMAN
McGill University, Montréal

CAMBRIDGE
UNIVERSITY PRESS

Shaftesbury Road, Cambridge CB2 8EA, United Kingdom

One Liberty Plaza, 20th Floor, New York, NY 10006, USA

477 Williamstown Road, Port Melbourne, VIC 3207, Australia

314–321, 3rd Floor, Plot 3, Splendor Forum, Jasola District Centre, New Delhi – 110025, India

103 Penang Road, #05–06/07, Visioncrest Commercial, Singapore 238467

Cambridge University Press is part of Cambridge University Press & Assessment, a department of the University of Cambridge.

We share the University's mission to contribute to society through the pursuit of education, learning and research at the highest international levels of excellence.

www.cambridge.org
Information on this title: www.cambridge.org/9781316511770

DOI: 10.1017/9781009053839

© Cambridge University Press & Assessment 2025

This publication is in copyright. Subject to statutory exception and to the provisions of relevant collective licensing agreements, no reproduction of any part may take place without the written permission of Cambridge University Press & Assessment.

When citing this work, please include a reference to the DOI 10.1017/9781009053839

First published 2025

A catalogue record for this publication is available from the British Library

Library of Congress Cataloging-in-Publication Data
NAMES: Klorman, Edward, 1982– author.
TITLE: Bach : the cello suites / Edward Klorman.
DESCRIPTION: [1.] | New York : Cambridge University Press, 2025. | Series: New Cambridge music handbooks | Includes bibliographical references and index.
IDENTIFIERS: LCCN 2024061779 | ISBN 9781316511770 (hardback) | ISBN 9781009054591 (paperback) | ISBN 9781009053839 (ebook)
SUBJECTS: LCSH: Bach, Johann Sebastian, 1685–1750. Suites, cello, BWV 1007–1012. | Bach, Johann Sebastian, 1685–1750. Violin music. | Bach, Johann Sebastian, 1685–1750 – Appreciation. | Stringed instrument music – 18th century – History and criticism.
CLASSIFICATION: LCC ML410.B13 K64 2025 | DDC 787.4/183092–dc23/eng/20241227
LC record available at https://lccn.loc.gov/2024061779

ISBN 978-1-316-51177-0 Hardback
ISBN 978-1-009-05459-1 Paperback

Cambridge University Press & Assessment has no responsibility for the persistence or accuracy of URLs for external or third-party internet websites referred to in this publication and does not guarantee that any content on such websites is, or will remain, accurate or appropriate.

For EU product safety concerns, contact us at Calle de José Abascal, 56, 1°, 28003 Madrid, Spain, or email eugpsr@cambridge.org

CONTENTS

List of Figures	*page* vi
List of Tables	viii
List of Music Examples	ix
Preface	xiii
Acknowledgments	xvi

1. Contexts: Cöthen, French Style, "Opus" Collections, and the Cello — 1
2. Dance Types, Preludes, and Analytical Perspectives — 33
3. The Four Manuscript Copies — 62
4. Transmission, Performance, and Reception: 1720–c. 1900 — 80
5. Transmission, Performance, and Reception: After c. 1900 — 115

Bibliography — 150
Index — 166

FIGURES

1.1 Figure playing viola da spalla (inhabited initial *page* 19 "P" for "prelude"). From Giuseppe Torelli, *Concertino per camera a violin e violoncello* (Bologna, c. 1687), violoncello partbook (detail). Reproduced by permission of the Bibliothèque nationale de France.

1.2 Figure playing viola da spalla. From *Procession de la* 20 *Fête-Dieu à Aix-en-Provence* (c. 1710–40). Screen, oil on wood (detail). Reproduced by permission of the City of Aix-en-Provence and P. Biolatto.

1.3 Giovanni Battista Sintes and Arnold van 21 Westerhout, engraving labeled "Viola," after illustration by Stefano Sparigioni. From Filippo Bonanni, *Gabinetto armonico* (Rome, 1722). Reproduced by permission of the Bodleian Library.

1.4 Bernard Picart, figure playing cello (1704). Etching 22 (detail). Reproduced by permission of the Rijksmuseum.

1.5 Thomas Gainsborough, *The Rev. John Chafy* 23 *Playing the Violoncello in a Landscape* (c. 1750–52). Oil on canvas (detail). Reproduced by permission of Tate Images.

1.6 Attributed to Charles Philips, *Portrait* 24 *of a Gentleman with a Violoncello* (c. 1720). Oil on canvas (detail), present whereabouts unknown. Reproduced by permission of Bridgeman Images.

1.7 Jean-Jacques Flipart, engraving of violoncello 25 player. Frontispiece to Michel Corrette, *Méthode théorique et pratique pour apprendre en peu de tems le violoncelle dans sa perfection* (Paris, 1741) (detail). Reproduced by permission of the Bibliothèque nationale de France.

List of Figures

5.1 Pablo Casals. Photo by Yousuf Karsh © 1954, reproduced by permission. 116

5.2 Cellist Mstislav Rostropovich plays Bach at Checkpoint Charlie (Berlin), November 11, 1989. Reproduced by permission of Action Press. 118

5.3 Augustus John, *Madame Suggia* (1920–23). Oil on canvas. Reproduced by permission of Tate Images and the Estate of Augustus John. 125

5.4 Lillian Fuchs. Photo by James Abresch (c. 1950). Reproduced by permission of the Juilliard Archives and Amédée Williams. 126

5.5 Yo-Yo Ma with local drummers in Dakar (Senegal), part of his thirty-six-city tour for *The Bach Project*. Photo by Austin Mann © 2020, reproduced by permission. 135

5.6 Dancer Eno Peçi and cellist Ditta Rohmann perform Jerome Robbins's *A Suite of Dances* (1994). Photo by Ashley Taylor © 2021. Reproduced by permission of the Robbins Rights Trust and the Vienna State Ballet. 140

TABLES

1.1 Layout of the Violin Solos and Cello Suites.   *page* 13

MUSIC EXAMPLES

1.1 Sieur de Machy, *Pièces de violle* (Paris, 1685), *page* 6
Gavotte en rondeau. Reproduced by permission of the Bibliothèque nationale de France.

1.2 Solo music with chordal models representing hand shapes.   17
   a. Johann Georg Pisendel, Sonata for unaccompanied violin, Allegro.
   b. Suite No. 3 in C Major, Prelude.

1.3 Suite No. 5, Prelude, fugue subject as compound melody.   18

2.1 Suite No. 3 in C Major, Allemande, double cadence.   35

2.2 Suite No. 5 in C Minor, Courante, hemiola effects.   36

2.3 Sarabandes, emphasis on second beats.   38
   a. Suite No. 1 in G Major.
   b. Suite No. 3 in C Major.
   c. Suite No. 5 in C Minor.

2.4 Suite No. 1, Menuet I, two-bar units (*pas de menuet*).   39

2.5 Suite No. 3 in C Major, Bourrées I and II, "dactylic" rhythm.   40

2.6 Suite No. 6 in D Major, Gavottes I and II, phrase counting after Edward Aldwell.   41
   a. Gavotte I.
   b. Gavotte II.

2.7 Two styles of gigues.   42
   a. Suite No. 6 in D Major: Italian giga (brilliant style).
   b. Suite No. 5 in C Minor: French gigue.

2.8 Suite No. 1 in G Major, harmonic motive.   44

2.9 Suite No. 3 in C Major, c′ to C scalar motive.   45

2.10 Suite No. 4 in E♭ Major, emphasis on D♭.   46

2.11 Suite No. 2 in D Minor, emphasis on Neapolitan harmony (E♭ major).   46

List of Music Examples

2.12 Suite No. 1 in G Major, Prelude, modified pattern prelude.   49
a. Opening pattern.
b. Freer material.

2.13 Suite No. 4 in E♭ Major, Prelude, figured-bass reduction.   51

2.14 *Niederfallen* figure: descending three-note arpeggio symbolizing Christ on the Mount of Olives.   53
a. Suite No. 4 in E♭ Major, Prelude.
b. *St. Matthew Passion*, recitative ("The Savior falls down before his Father").
c. Heinrich Ignaz Franz Biber, Mystery Sonata No. 6 ("Christ on the Mount of Olives").

3.1 Suite No. 1 in G Major, Prelude: The four manuscript copies. Reproduced by permission of the Berlin State Library and the Austrian National Library.   63
a. Anna Magdalena Bach (Source A).
b. Johann Peter Kellner (Source B).
c. Johann Nikolaus Schober (Source C, first half).
d. Anonymous Hamburg copyist (Source D).

3.2 Violin Solos, comparing slurs in manuscripts by J. S. Bach and Anna Magdalena Bach. Reproduced by permission of the Berlin State Library.   66
a. Sonata No. 1 in G Minor, Adagio (m. 6).
b. Partita No. 1 in B Minor, Tempo di Borea (m. 58).
c. Sonata No. 2 in A Minor, Andante (m. 9).
d. Partita No. 2 in D minor, Allemande (m. 2).

3.3 Suite No. 2 in D Minor, Menuet I, variant readings in mm. 6–7.   73

4.1 Suite No. 1 in G Major, Gigue, syncopated ties as edited by Louis-Pierre Norblin. Reproduced by permission of the Music and Theater Library of Sweden.   86

4.2 Justus Johann Friedrich Dotzauer, two passages marked with *portamento* fingerings.   89
a. Suite No. 1 in G Major, Menuet II.
b. Suite No. 2 in D Minor, Sarabande.

List of Music Examples

4.3 Chords as renotated in Friedrich Grützmacher's "original" edition. — 97
 a. Suite No. 1 in G Major, Sarabande.
 b. Suite No. 5 in C Minor, Allemande.
 c. Suite No. 6 in D Major, Sarabande.

4.4 Suite No. 1 in G Major, Courante, comparing Friedrich Grützmacher's "concert" and "original" editions. — 99

4.5 Suite No. 1 in G Major, Prelude, as edited by Hugo Becker. Reproduced by permission of McGill University. — 101

4.6 Suite No. 6 in D Major, Gavotte II, as arranged by W. H. Squire. — 105

5.1 Minor variants, as recorded by Pablo Casals. — 121
 a. Suite No. 1 in G Major, Gigue.
 b. Suite No. 2 in D Minor, Allemande.
 c. Suite No. 3 in C Major, Bourrée I.

5.2 Suite No. 2 in D Minor, Prelude, as edited by Diran Alexanian. Reproduced by permission of Riemenschneider Bach Institute, Baldwin Wallace University. — 122

5.3 *Bariolage* figures performed as double stops by Pablo Casals. — 124
 a. Suite No. 2 in D Minor, Courante.
 b. Suite No. 3 in C Major, Gigue.

5.4 Suite No. 6 in D Major, Courante, as analyzed by Ernst Kurth. — 129

5.5 Suite No. 2 in D Minor, Prelude (climax), as analyzed by Ernst Kurth. — 129

PREFACE

Like many string players, I first encountered music arranged from J. S. Bach's Cello Suites during my first year of lessons. I began studying the Cello Suites in earnest as a teenager, and I have never stopped exploring their musical and technical challenges. This handbook examines how these thirty-six remarkable pieces came to be foundational to the training repertoire for cello and why they today occupy such a special place in our musical culture.

Whereas Bach was inheritor to an important German tradition of unaccompanied violin music, it is not at all obvious why he chose to compose in this style for the cello. This book offers some context about Bach's creative activities around the time he composed the Cello Suites that allows us to speculate. I proceed in a spiral form, beginning with musicians in Bach's immediate circle c. 1720, gradually expanding outward to a broader array of German musical writers and critics, and finally following the Cello Suites' reception across Europe and eventually around the world, influencing musicians, artists, and a global public well beyond the "classical" music sphere. I devote special attention to the often-overlooked record of public performances before Pablo Casals's world-premiere recordings from the late 1930s. In recounting that history, we witness the surprising variety of interpretive approaches adopted by the first generations of musicians to grapple seriously with the Cello Suites.

Although this book focuses specifically on the Cello Suites, Bach's Sonatas and Partitas for Solo Violin (or "Violin Solos") are mentioned frequently. Indeed, there would have been compelling reasons for this study to consider the Violin Solos and Cello Suites together, since Bach conceived them jointly as a two-part collection. Nevertheless, since there are already several volumes devoted specifically to the Violin Solos, the Cello Suites deserve a dedicated study. Whereas we can definitively answer many essential questions about the Violin Solos – such as their date of completion, the exact type of instrument for which they were composed, the earliest musicians to perform them, the whereabouts of their autograph manuscript, and precisely which notes and articulations Bach wrote – those issues all remain murky with respect to the Cello Suites. This book shows how information known about the Violin Solos can support educated guesses about the Cello Suites, even if such speculation necessarily remains inconclusive.

The absence of a surviving autograph manuscript of the Cello Suites has been a source of romance and mystery – as well as of frustration for cellists and editors. Pathbreaking research by Andrew Talle (discussed in Chapter 3) explains the most likely reason why the autograph has disappeared and challenges the long-standing, widespread belief that Anna Magdalena Bach's manuscript copy should be considered as a kind of "surrogate" autograph. All citations of Talle's edition of the Cello Suites (Bärenreiter, 2018) refer specifically to the revised preface of its third printing, which appeared in 2022 but bears a copyright date of 2018.

Discussions of the Cello Suites can be complicated by unexamined beliefs and opinions that are too often presented as facts. During my years as a viola student, I encountered a bewilderingly wide range of contradictory ideas about the "correct" way to perform the Cello Suites. In this handbook, I have endeavored to cut through the noise by presenting reliable information grounded in evidence. Rather than foregrounding my own personal preferences, I have focused on separating received myths from verifiable information and illustrating historical contexts that shed light on the available evidence. This approach, I believe, empowers readers to approach the Cello Suites from an informed position.

As this book is written for an anglophone readership, I cite historical sources in published English translations where possible. In other cases, translations are my own unless indicated otherwise. I primarily cite English-language secondary sources, even as I admire the tremendous body of Bach scholarship in other languages (especially German). I have retained variant spellings (such as "Suonaten" and "Suitten") as they appear in historical

Preface

sources, with two exceptions: "bouree" and "gique" are given respectively as "bourrée" and "gigue." I use historical German forms such as "Capellmeister" and "Cöthen," which today are spelled with a *K*.

References to "Bach" by default indicate J. S. Bach. Other members of his family are consistently given with full names. All examples are from Bach's Cello Suites, unless otherwise indicated. With the exception of editions of Bach's Cello Suites, citations of items dating from before 1900 omit publisher information. All Bach editions are listed in the Bibliography under their editors or arrangers, rather than under "Bach." Since many historical editions are difficult to date precisely, dates should be understood as estimates.

Facsimiles of all manuscripts and many historical editions discussed in this book can be viewed on the Internet Music Score Library Project (http://imslp.org). Manuscript sources can also be viewed on Bach Digital (http://bach-digital.de). Examples from Suite No. 5 are generally given at sounding pitch, not in the original *scordatura* notation. References to "Suite No. 1" indicate *Cello* Suite No. 1 (BWV1007), as opposed to any other Bach suite. I omit BWV numbers for very familiar compositions but include them for pieces that may be less well known. When precision is needed about pitches in specific registers, I adopt the traditional (Helmholtz) system, where the cello's open strings are designated C–G–d–a and where middle C is c′.

A discography of Bach Cello Suites recordings, compiled by Charles Pidsley and Mark Siner, is available at http://bachcellosuites.co.uk. Albums cited in this book are included in the Bibliography under the names of the (principal) performer. Pablo Casals's best-known recordings of the Cello Suites are the complete cycle recorded 1936–39, but this book also mentions his other studio and live recordings. Full discographic information for Casals's recordings is available at www.paucasals.org/en/discography and is not provided in the notes or Bibliography.

ACKNOWLEDGMENTS

This book was made possible through the support of many wonderful people and institutions. My research was funded by grants from the Fonds de recherche du Québec – Société et culture and the Canada Research Chairs program. McGill University provided a sabbatical leave and other teaching release that enabled me to devote time to research and writing. I am enormously grateful to Cathy Martin at McGill's Marvin Duchow Music Library and to the interlibrary loan staff for assistance tracking down dozens of hard-to-find resources. I also benefited from a visit to the Riemenschneider Bach Institute, where Christina Fuhrmann and Paul Cary enabled me to consult rare editions. I am grateful to Núria Ballester and Bernard Meillat of the Pau Casals Foundation for providing information and support. Philomeen Lelieveldt, curator of the collections of the Netherlands Music Institute, provided background about Gerrit Hulshoff, author of the first known monograph on Bach's Cello Suites.

To my extraordinary research assistants – Philipp Elssner and Shanti Nachtergaele – I owe a debt of gratitude for their dedication and meticulous care. Having such brilliant performer-scholars as collaborators on this project was a great joy and enriched this book immensely. Andrew Talle was uncommonly generous with his expertise about manuscript sources and critical editing; Chapter 3 is largely a report on the findings of his recent work on the manuscript sources. George Kennaway and Martin Barré – both experts on historical cellists – kindly consulted with me about early editions of the Cello Suites and about Pablo Casals. Junah Chung and Amédée Daryl Williams provided information about their viola teacher, Lillian Fuchs. Kuramochi Fumiyo and Allen Lieb shared insights about the repertoire included in the Suzuki violin curriculum.

Acknowledgments

Anonymous contributors to forums on Reddit and WhoSampled.com led me to fascinating examples of pop culture influenced by Bach's Cello Suites. Bruce Alan Brown offered extensive advice about eighteenth-century historical materials. David Bynog kindly assisted with many stylistic and bibliographic matters. I have benefited from the advice of several expert colleagues who have assisted me with rendering sometimes unwieldy historical texts into English. I am grateful for advice on German translations from Harald Krebs, William Rothstein, and Liza Stepanova; on French material from Bruce Alan Brown and Marie-Ève Piché; and on Dutch material from Shanti Nachtergaele.

Dorian Bandy and Joseph N. Straus offered valuable feedback on an early draft. I also benefited from suggestions from Stuart Cheney, Marianne Dumas, Katharine Ellis, Elinor Frey, Ara Guzelimian, Robert L. Marshall, Markus Neuwirth, Nathan Pell, Tully Potter, Derek Remeš, David Schulenberg, Lloyd Whitesell, and Christoph Wolff. I am solely responsible for all errors and faults in this book.

I wish to express my gratitude to the team at Cambridge University Press, especially to series editor Nicole Grimes and music editor Kate Brett. Thank you to the anonymous peer reviewer, to Lisa Sinclair for copy editing, and to Nigel Graves for overseeing the production process. Music examples were expertly typeset by Michael Durnin, and figures were prepared by Krystyna Oakman and Samantha Youssef.

I am grateful for my family, whose support has enabled me to pursue my love of music – and of Bach in particular – over many years. To my husband, Young Guen: Your love and encouragement during the intense final stages of research and writing have made all the difference.

This book is dedicated to Heidi and Libba, in gratitude for your ever-inspiring teaching, about viola playing and about life.

I

CONTEXTS: CÖTHEN, FRENCH STYLE, "OPUS" COLLECTIONS, AND THE CELLO

J. S. Bach's Cello Suites were most likely completed, like his Violin Solos ("Sonatas and Partitas"), around the middle of his tenure as Capellmeister and director of chamber music for Prince Leopold of Anhalt-Cöthen (1694–1728). Since Leopold's reformed Calvinist court chapel did not require elaborate church music or organ playing, Bach's responsibilities during his Cöthen period (1717–23) centered around composing instrumental music and secular cantatas to satisfy his patron's demand for musical divertissements. A devoted music enthusiast, Leopold sang and played harpsichord, violin, and viol (also known as viola da gamba).[1]

Despite the traditional portrait of Bach as an industrious, disciplined musician and teacher, he did not always get on well with his various employers.[2] Yet he enjoyed a notably good rapport with Leopold, who was nine years his junior. The prince paid Bach handsomely, showcased his talents during two trips to the fashionable spa in Carlsbad (Bohemia), and was godfather to his son Leopold Augustus (1718–19), suggesting a personal dimension to their relationship.[3] Even after financial and other personal circumstances led Leopold to scale back musical activities at his court, prompting Bach to seek other employment in Leipzig, the composer nevertheless retained the title of Capellmeister in Cöthen on a nonresident basis for the rest of the prince's life. Bach's devotion to his princely patron is evinced by his regular return visits to perform in Cöthen, usually together with Anna Magdalena Bach (1701–60), the last of which was to provide music for Leopold's state funeral in 1729. In a letter written the following year, Bach reminisced fondly about his time in Cöthen: "There I had a gracious Prince, who both loved and knew music, and in his service I intended to spend the rest of my life."[4] Bach's assessment was echoed some decades later by composer Johann Adam Hiller (1728–1804): "This Prince Leopold was a great connoisseur and champion of music; he himself played the violin not badly and sang a good bass."[5]

In its focus on secular music, the Cöthen position was unique among the posts Bach held throughout his career. Compared to his more extensive duties as court organist and chamber musician in Weimar (1708–17) and especially as cantor and music director in Leipzig (1723–50), the lighter responsibilities in Cöthen afforded Bach the time, flexibility, and creative freedom to complete some of his most ambitious instrumental projects, including not only the highly original music for solo violin and cello but also the French Suites, the first book of the *Well-Tempered Clavier*, and the Brandenburg Concertos.[6] Moreover, in the musicians of the Cöthen court Capelle, he had access to some of the finest performers he could have hoped for. A core group of eight soloists (plus Bach as Capellmeister), all distinguished virtuosos, lived in close proximity in the small town, rehearsing and performing together regularly, and their numbers were reinforced by additional ripienists (string section members) and guests when a larger ensemble was needed.

The Capelle's serious rehearsal practices were unusual enough to receive special comment in a 1722 report by the cantor of Cöthen's St. Jacobi Church: "The princely Capelle in this town, which week in week out holds its *Exercitium musicum*, makes an example that even the most famous virtuosos rehearse and exercise their pieces together beforehand."[7] This lauding account suggests a high artistic standard for the Capelle, and the members' close working relationships seem to have fostered some lasting personal connections. Although much of the ensemble music Bach composed in Cöthen does not survive, it must have been a remarkably fertile period, owing to Leopold's enthusiasm about and investment in musical life at his court, as well as to the inspiration of the outstanding musicians of the Capelle.[8]

Le Goût Français at German Courts

Although Bach never traveled to France, French manners, music, and dance were part of his upbringing and of the cultural atmosphere at Cöthen as he composed the Cello Suites. Leopold's court

Le Goût Français at German Courts

included French paintings and tapestries and an orangery on the castle grounds.[9] During Bach's lifetime, the instrumental dance suite was understood in Germany largely as a French import. Whereas suites for unaccompanied cello were not an established genre among German composers, bass viol suites in the French tradition (*pièces de viole*) were almost certainly present at Cöthen and may in part have inspired Bach's conception of the Cello Suites.[10]

One could not overstate the role of French dance masters as the most important tastemakers at German courts, with an influence that extended beyond dance and music to manners, social rituals, and fashion. A well-known (satirical) representation of a Parisian dance master providing instruction in both dance and manners is found in Molière's *Le Bourgeois Gentilhomme* (1670). Pierre Rameau (1674–1748), dance master to the Queen of Spain, explained:

> We can say, to the glory of our nation, that it has a true gift for beautiful dancing. Far from denying this, nearly all foreigners have, for nearly a century, come to admire our dances [and] to educate themselves at our performances and in our schools. There is hardly a court in Europe that does not have a dancing master from our nation.[11]

The appointment of Parisian dance masters and other musicians in many German courts brought about both the diffusion of French music through manuscript copies and printed parts and performance of French or French-inspired music, dance, and theater.[12]

Bach was first introduced to French music, dance, and courtly culture as a teenager in Lüneburg, where he was a choral scholar at St. Michael's Latin School (1700–1702). Bach sang in the Matins choir with students from the adjacent *Ritter-Academie*, an elite school for noble youth, where French was the obligatory spoken language, where students had daily lessons in French language, dancing, and etiquette, and where entertainments included French theater and ballet.[13] Bach almost certainly had contact with the dance master of the *Ritter-Academie*, Thomas de la Selle (dates unknown), a pupil of Jean-Baptiste Lully (1632–87) and a violinist at the French-styled ducal court of Celle. The renowned Celle Capelle was an ensemble of twenty-four musicians modeled after Lully's orchestra at Versailles.[14] Bach's obituary states that

3

hearing that "then famous band ... consisting for the most part of Frenchmen ... [afforded him] a thorough grounding in the French taste, which, in those regions, was at the time something quite new."[15] Since Bach himself was likely the ultimate source of this account, it would seem that his youthful introduction to French music and manners had made a lasting impression.

The infatuation of German princes with French courtly culture stemmed from the division of the Holy Roman Empire into some 300 small, sovereign principalities after the Thirty Years' War (1618–48). Princes "with small domains and large ambitions ... did everything conceivable to create a miniature Versailles at [their] court[s],"[16] including by cultivating French language and manners and by mounting festivities that aspired toward the grandeur of those of Louis XIV (the "Sun King," 1638–1715).[17] German princes learned French from a young age and studied both dance and comportment with Parisian dance masters.

Leopold had cultivated French manners – including the language, dance, riding, fencing, and music – as a student at the Berlin *Ritter-Academie* (1707–10).[18] At the time, musical life at the Prussian court in Berlin had become highly Gallicized under the influence of the dance master and concertmaster Jean-Baptiste Volumier (c. 1670–1728). Steeped in an opulent French cultural environment, the teenage Leopold must have been a devoted dance student since, in 1708–9, he and his younger brother performed among the "Dancers in the Entrée of the Amours and Plaisirs" in a magnificent opera produced for the royal wedding.[19]

Leopold's grand tour, undertaken in 1710–13, reflected his devotion to music. He attended numerous opera performances; acquired a considerable amount of sheet music, including rare scores by Lully and Francesco Mancini (1672–1737); rented harpsichords in several locations; and engaged composer Johann David Heinichen (1683–1729) to join for a seven-month stretch of the journey.[20] In 1713, while he was still on his tour, a rare opportunity arose for Leopold to significantly expand and enhance the Cöthen Capelle when he learned of the abrupt dissolution of the Prussian court Capelle in Berlin, an "act of cultural barbarism" committed by Friedrich Wilhelm I (the "Soldier King," 1688–1740) just after his ascent to the throne.[21] Leopold persuaded his mother

Le Goût Français at German Courts

(then governing as regent) to hire several of the leading Berlin musicians, six of whom arrived in Cöthen soon after, with the cellist Christian Bernhard Linike (1673–1751) joining in 1716. In a shrewd maneuver, Leopold thus transformed the Cöthen Capelle into one that, in its size and virtuosity, rivaled those of many larger, more established courts.

Given Leopold's fondness for the viol, he must have been particularly pleased with the appointment of Christian Ferdinand Abel (c. 1683–1737), one of the finest German viol players, to the Cöthen Capelle around 1714. Having grown up at the French-styled court at Celle, where he probably served as a court musician, Abel was an accomplished virtuoso in the French viol tradition. His service at Cöthen afforded Leopold not only the pleasure of his performances but also opportunities to play with and to learn from him on the instrument.[22] Bach's three viol sonatas (BWV 1027–29) were likely composed for Abel to play for or teach to Leopold.

It has long been speculated that Abel may have been the first performer of Bach's Cello Suites, given his close friendship with Bach.[23] This theory is difficult to support, given the lack of evidence that Abel played the cello – besides his primary background as a viol player, Cöthen court records show him as a violinist – and moreover considering the presence at Cöthen of the excellent cellist Linike. On the other hand, Abel may have influenced the conception of the Cello Suites in a different way. German viol players such as Abel and Leopold were inheritors to an extensive and venerable tradition of *pièces de viole* – collections of preludes, dance movements, and character pieces for bass viol, a repertoire that flourished in France and that was imitated extensively by German and Dutch composers. Example 1.1 reproduces a gavotte en rondeau by Sieur de Machy (fl. c. 1660–90), an avid proponent of the viol as a solo (unaccompanied) instrument. In this piece, the viol conveys both melody and harmony, sometimes through chords and double stops, as well as through registral leaps that distinguish the bass line from upper voices.

The French viol player Jean Rousseau (1644–99) described these features as the "harmonic" style (*jeu d'harmonie*) of viol playing, as opposed to the "melodic" style (*jeu de mélodie*), in which the

Example 1.1 Sieur de Machy, *Pièces de violle* (Paris, 1685), Gavotte en rondeau. Reproduced by permission of the Bibliothèque nationale de France.

viol simply plays the tune and requires extrinsic accompaniment.[24] Whereas Rousseau advocated the melodic style, de Machy considered a viol player playing only melodies to be comparable to "a man who plays perfectly on the harpsichord or organ, [but] only with one hand."[25] In practice, the distinction between the two styles was sometimes blurred, as some collections were composed to be playable either solo or with basso continuo accompaniment. Music in the *pièces de viole* tradition – either by French composers or by Dutch and German composers who inherited and extended it – was very likely part of the musical atmosphere at Cöthen,[26] considering that Leopold and Abel were both viol players whose musical sensibilities had been shaped in French-influenced courts.[27]

The "harmonic" style of viol playing broadly resembles the texture of Bach's Cello Suites, which combine melody, harmony, and bass line in a similar way (compare Example 1.1 to the Gavotte I from Suite No. 6, shown in Example 2.6a). At the time Bach composed the Cello Suites, the cello – a member of the Italianate violin family – was a comparatively newer instrument than the illustrious French viol. Lacking a robust tradition of unaccompanied music, the cello was best known north of the Alps as an instrument suitable for bass lines in ensemble music,[28] although one poised to grow in popularity as the viol was beginning to decline and as Italian instrumental music was gaining in prestige in German-speaking lands.²⁹ Although seventeenth-century Bolognese cellists had composed for cellos tuned C–G–d–g (as in Bach's Suite No. 5), including Domenico Gabrielli's Ricercari for unaccompanied cello (1689), it is doubtful that this music would have been familiar to Bach or could have served as his prototype.³⁰ On the other hand, bass viol playing exerted a clear influence on early cello techniques and repertoires. Given the cross-pollination between these instruments, it is entirely possible that Abel's presence at Cöthen, and Leopold's presumed penchant for *pièces de viole* and for French courtly and theatrical dance, may have inspired Bach to experiment with transposing the solo-viol tradition into suites for unaccompanied cello.

Bach's Violin Solos and Cello Suites as "Opus" Collections

Starting during his appointment in Weimar (1708–17) and continuing in Cöthen (1717–23), Bach assembled some of his most impressive and original instrumental compositions into manuscript collections possessing what Christoph Wolff has called "opus character."³¹ Although just a handful of Bach's compositions were published during his lifetime – and he assigned a literal opus number only once (to the *Clavier-Übung* I, published in 1731 as "opus 1") – various unpublished sets also stand out as touchstone collections, often comprising six pieces that were conceived or assembled with particular care and to which Bach attached special importance. Once these collections were polished into their final versions, Bach penned them in fair copies.

These "opus" collections aspire toward an encyclopedic ideal, as if Bach sought to reveal exhaustively the range of compositional possibilities of certain genres and instrumental forces. Musicians who play the six Brandenburg Concertos, for instance, encounter a variety of traditional and novel instrumental combinations, with many passages testing the limits of the soloists' technique and with each piece instantiating the genre of *concerto grosso* in a different way. Likewise, a keyboard player who studies either book of the *Well-Tempered Clavier* will have Bach as a guide through a complete survey of all twenty-four major and minor keys, exploring a variety of styles and textures in preludes and contrapuntal techniques in the fugues. Such collections are not only a means for musicians to develop and display their virtuosity as instrumentalists; they are, moreover, demonstrations of Bach's virtuosity as a composer.

The earliest writings to discuss Bach's Violin Solos and Cello Suites in these terms are by his son Carl Philipp Emanuel (1714–88) and his student Johann Friedrich Agricola (1720–74), whose coauthored obituary of the elder Bach was published in 1754. Comprising a brief overview of his life and works, the obituary includes a list summarizing his published and unpublished music, mostly detailing vocal, organ, and other keyboard music. The list of unpublished music also includes "six sonatas for the violin, without [accompanying] bass," "six of the same for the violoncello," and finally "a mass of other instrumental pieces of all sorts and for all kinds of music."[32] The obituary is slightly imprecise as to the genres of these collections: alternating church sonatas and partitas for solo violin and suites for solo cello. That these pieces were the only non-keyboard instrumental works singled out for special mention illustrates that the authors – and probably the composer himself – regarded them as extraordinary achievements comparable to his most notable works in the genres for which he was best known (vocal, organ, and keyboard).[33] C. P. E. Bach owned a manuscript copy of the Cello Suites, which he kept his whole life and of which he commissioned at least one copy (see discussion of Source C in Chapters 3 and 4).

Two decades later, C. P. E. Bach corresponded extensively with his father's biographer Johann Nikolaus Forkel (1749–1818). In an oft-cited letter describing his father's artistic traits, C. P. E. Bach wrote:

He heard the slightest wrong note even in the largest combinations. As the greatest expert and judge of harmony, he liked best to play the viola, with appropriate loudness and softness. In his youth, and until the approach of old age, he played the violin cleanly and penetratingly, and thus kept the orchestra in better order than he could have done with the harpsichord. He understood to perfection the possibilities of all stringed instruments. This is evidenced by his solos for the violin and for the violoncello without [accompanying] bass. One of the greatest violinists told me once that he had seen nothing more perfect for learning to be a good violinist, and could suggest nothing better to anyone eager to learn, than the said violin solos without bass.[34]

Although during his lifetime Bach was best known as an organ and keyboard virtuoso and only secondarily as a composer, this account emphasizes his intimate knowledge of string instruments. Bach had played the violin from a young age, almost certainly having picked it up as a child through his father, Johann Ambrosius, an accomplished violinist from whom Bach probably inherited his Stainer violin.[35] According to C. P. E. Bach's letter, his father's expertise with string instruments was manifest not only in his masterful playing but also in his unaccompanied music for violin and cello, which explored those instruments to their full capacities.

Forkel likewise singled out the Violin Solos and Cello Suites for special mention in his 1802 biography of Bach. Noting that Bach composed concertos and other solo pieces for a wide variety of instruments, he observed that the composer "always contrived them so that his performers could, by their means, improve on their instruments."[36] He held that the Violin Solos and Cello Suites made up for the many instrumental pieces that had not survived, adding (in a gloss on C. P. E. Bach's aforementioned letter): "For a long series of years, the violin solos were universally considered by the greatest performers on the violin as the best means to make an ambitious student a perfect master of his instrument. The solos for the violoncello are, in this respect, of equal value."[37] Forkel's remarks were prescient as these pieces have since become central to the training repertoire for violinists and cellists. They are among the most frequently performed and recorded music for both instruments.

Bach's Violin Solos and Cello Suites were conceived together as a two-part collection. Scholars have made various speculations as to their chronology, but there are good reasons to presume that the violin pieces were composed first.[38] Since the complexity and originality of the Violin Solos suggest an extended gestation period, one might surmise that Bach probably began the set in Weimar. Although his primary Weimar post was as court organist, Bach also served as chamber musician and, after 1714, was promoted to concertmaster, roles that would have included both harpsichord and violin playing. It was during this period that Bach first showed an interest in the violin as a virtuoso, polyphonic instrument. His oldest surviving chamber music, the Fugue in G Minor for Violin and Continuo (BWV 1026), was composed in Weimar and illustrates his development of virtuoso violin technique including complex double stops and polyphony.

Whenever he may have begun working on the Violin Solos, he finished by 1720, when he copied them out in an extraordinarily neat, calligraphic manuscript. Containing virtually no errors, corrections, or other signs of creative deliberation, that manuscript is clearly a fair copy made from earlier composing drafts. Such ornate, tidy manuscripts date only from the Cöthen period, when Bach's relatively light duties permitted him to take such care with fair copies.[39] The aesthetic beauty of this manuscript also reflects the value the composer attached to the Violin Solos.

Bach undertook the copying work for the Violin Solos while visiting the Carlsbad spa in May–July 1720 as a member of Leopold's entourage. Since the autograph is written on paper manufactured nearby in Joachimsthal (Bohemia), Bach must have acquired the paper and begun the copying work during the extended trip.[40] The manuscript's title page is dated 1720 and bears the designation "Libro Primo," suggesting that the Cello Suites were already well underway (if not complete) and that their fair copy was presumably planned as the "Libro Secondo." However, to the great consternation of cellists worldwide, no such autograph manuscript is extant – neither a fair copy nor a composing draft.

Wolff offers a plausible explanation for the absence of an autograph fair copy. When Bach made his final copy of the Violin Solos in Carlsbad during spring 1720, the Cello Suites may well have been complete in draft form, ready to be copied into their final version (the would-be "Libro Secondo"). But Bach soon returned to Cöthen only to receive the shocking news that Maria Barbara Bach (1684–1720), his wife of almost thirteen years and mother of his first seven children, had died and been buried during his extended absence. This sudden personal tragedy was a devastating disruption for the Bach family. In the face of more pressing matters – including, just four months later, a long journey to Hamburg to give an organ concert as a candidate for a position at St. Jacobi Church[41] – it may be that he never found the time to return to the project of creating a fair copy of the Cello Suites comparable to that of the Violin Solos. If this speculation is correct, and Bach only ever notated the Cello Suites in a draft, composing score – one lacking the neatness and clarity of a fair copy – that would partly explain the discrepancies and inconsistencies among manuscript copies made by other scribes (see Chapter 3).[42]

Even if Bach's (presumed) plan for "sibling" fair copies of the Violin Solos and Cello Suites never came to fruition, their status as companion collections is confirmed by a manuscript copy written by Anna Magdalena Bach c. 1727–31 that combined both collections into a two-part manuscript made at the behest of violinist Georg Heinrich Ludwig Schwanberger (1696–1774), who studied with Bach in Leipzig in 1727–28 (see discussion of Source A in Chapter 3). A title page in Schwanberger's hand designates the Cello Suites as "Pars 2" and bears the title "6 | Suites a | Violoncello Solo | senza | Basso | composées | par | Sr J. S. Bach. | Maitre de Chapelle." Tellingly, "Maître de Chapelle" is the French equivalent of Bach's Cöthen title ("Capellmeister"), which points to the Cello Suites having been completed there rather than in Leipzig.[43] Bach similarly identified himself as "Maître de Chapelle" on the autograph of the Brandenburg Concertos, completed in Cöthen in 1721.

Some scholars have speculated that the Cello Suites (or at least Suite No. 6) might have been composed after Bach arrived in Leipzig, given his interest in five-string instruments in the years after he settled there.[44] Around 1723, Bach worked with the Leipzig luthier Johann Christian Hofmann (1683–1750) to design a five-string instrument held on the shoulder called "viola pomposa." In the ensuing years, he composed about a dozen cantatas that included an instrument designated "violoncello piccolo," which in some cases appears to refer to a five-string instrument. Despite the apparent similarity between these instruments and the one that Suite No. 6 calls for, the relationship between the Cello Suites and the Leipzig cantatas is too oblique to override other compelling evidence that the Cello Suites were most likely composed in Cöthen.[45]

Bach's Plan for the Cello Suites

The close relationship between the Violin Solos and Cello Suites notwithstanding, they nevertheless contain different kinds of music, as shown in Table 1.1. Whereas the Violin Solos are eclectic in terms of both the number, types, and length of movements, the Cello Suites each comprise an opening prelude followed by five dances. Whereas the dance movements of the violin partitas use a mixture of French and Italian titles (e.g., gigue vs. giga or bourrée vs. borea), the Cello Suites consistently use French titles. The "core" dances of each suite all follow the same order: allemande, courante, sarabande, and gigue, the standard sequence for instrumental suites composed after c. 1670, as in examples from Dietrich Becker's *Musicalische Frühlings-Früchte* (Hamburg, 1668) and *Zwey-Stimmiger Sonaten und Suiten* (Hamburg, 1674), Johann Kuhnau's *Neuer Clavier-Übung* (Leipzig, 1689–92), Johann Caspar Ferdinand Fischer's *Musicalischer-Parnasus* (Augsburg, c. 1700), and Charles Dieupart's *Six suittes de clavessin* (Amsterdam, c. 1701).

Between the sarabande and gigue of each Cello Suite, Bach includes a pair of other dances performed *da capo*: menuets in Suites Nos. 1–2, bourrées in Suites Nos. 3–4, and gavottes in Suites Nos. 5–6. These paired dances were known as galanteries (*Galanterien*), a designation reflecting their more modern, fashionable status compared to the core dances of the Baroque suite, which were older and had become more stylized by Bach's lifetime. The distinction between the traditional core suite dances and the more modern galanteries is suggested by the title Bach used for the 1731 publication of his Partitas (BWV 825–30): *Clavir-Übung, Comprising Preludes, Allemandes, Courantes, Sarabandes, Gigues, Minuets, and Other Galanteries* [...].

In their number and order of movements, Bach's Cello Suites follow the model of his earliest major collection of keyboard suites, the six English Suites (completed in Cöthen but probably begun in Weimar),[46] which follow the pattern of Prelude–Allemande–Courante–Sarabande–[various galanteries]–Gigue. The Cello Suites adhere to a more regular plan for the type of galanteries, which tend to divide the cycle into three pairs of suites, grouping together the two with menuets, bourrées, and gavottes. The

Bach's Plan for the Cello Suites

Table 1.1 *Layout of the Violin Solos and Cello Suites.*

Violin Solos	Cello Suites
Sonata No. 1 in G Minor (BWV1001) Adagio Fuga: Allegro Siciliana Presto	**Suite No. 1 in G Major (BWV1007)** Prelude Allemande Courante Sarabande Menuet I–Menuet II (G minor) Gigue
Partita No. 1 in B Minor (BWV1002) Allemanda–Double Corrente–Double Sarabande–Double Tempo di Borea–Double	**Suite No. 2 in D Minor (BWV1008)** Prelude Allemande Courante Sarabande Menuet I–Menuet II (D major) Gigue
Sonata No. 2 in A Minor (BWV1003) Grave Fuga Andante Allegro	**Suite No. 3 in C Major (BWV1009)** Prelude Allemande Courante Sarabande Bourrée I–Bourrée II (C minor) Gigue
Partita No. 2 in D Minor (BWV1004) Allemanda Corrente Sarabanda Giga Ciaconna	**Suite No. 4 in E♭ Major (BWV1010)** Prelude Allemande Courante Sarabande Bourrée I–Bourrée II Gigue
Sonata No. 3 in C Major (BWV1005) Adagio Fuga Largo Allegro assai	**Suite No. 5 in C Minor (BWV1011)** *scordatura tuning:* **C–G–d–g** Prelude Allemande Courante Sarabande Gavotte I–Gavotte II Gigue
Partita No. 3 in E Major (BWV1006) Preludio Loure Gavotte en rondeau Menuet I–Menuet II Bourrée Gigue	**Suite No. 6 in D Major (BWV1012)** *five-string instrument:* **C–G–d–a–e′** Prelude Allemande Courante Sarabande Gavotte I–Gavotte II Gigue

organization into pairs of suites is further reinforced by the special cello tunings called for in Suites Nos. 5–6. Whereas the first four suites are composed for a cello with standard tuning in fifths (C–G–d–a), the Suite No. 5 calls for a *scordatura* tuning, with the top string tuned a whole step lower than usual (C–G–d–g), and Suite No. 6 is composed for a five-string instrument (tuned C–G–d–a–e′). The final pair of suites is therefore marked by the special sonorities and chord voicings afforded by the distinctive tunings. The inclusion of suites for an altered or extended cello aligns with C. P. E. Bach's and Forkel's observations about the collection cultivating a cellist's complete mastery of the instrument (in all its forms). Finally, unlike the Violin Solos, the Cello Suites are arranged approximately in ascending order of technical complexity, owing to challenges posed by the special tunings (Suites Nos. 5 and 6) and to the expanded range and brilliant passagework in Suite No. 6 in particular.

Cutting across the division of the cycle into three pairs of suites, it is also possible to conceive of the collection as two sets of three suites based on the key scheme: G–d–C (Suites Nos. 1–3) and E♭–c–D (Suites Nos. 4–6), where each trio of suites follows the pattern major–minor–major.[47] Moreover, Suites Nos. 1–3 all use parallel major/minor keys for the galanteries (i.e., a menuet I in G *major* paired with a menuet II in G *minor*, etc.), whereas Suites Nos. 4–6 maintain the same key and mode for all movements. In Suite No. 4, it would have been impractical to compose the Bourrée II in the remote key of E♭ minor (with six flats!). However, no such constraint would have prevented Bach from using parallel keys for the paired Gavottes of Suites No. 5 (in C minor) or No. 6 (in D major). In sum, compared to the more varied kinds of music found among the Violin Solos, the tighter organization of the cello collection and the arrangement as three pairs of suites (or possibly two trios of suites) suggest an overall plan for the six-suite cycle.

Bach and the Solo Violin

Bach's path from his early, organ-focused positions to more chamber-music-oriented roles in Weimar and Cöthen led to greater involvement with the violin. His near-exclusive focus on keyboard and organ music through around 1714 and his subsequent branching out to other instruments were, as Wolff observes, "related for the most part to changing official duties and self-chosen priorities" at his various major posts throughout his career: as town organist in Arnstadt (1703) and Mühlhausen (1707), then as court organist and chamber musician in Weimar (1708, with promotion to concertmaster in 1714), then as Capellmeister and director of chamber music in Cöthen (1717), and finally as cantor and music director in Leipzig (1723, where he later assumed additional duties as director of the Collegium Musicum).[48]

Whereas Bach was apparently the earliest German composer to explore the solo cello as a polyphonic instrument, in composing for solo violin he was following a well-trodden path. A significant tradition of contrapuntal solo music by violinist-composers in German-speaking lands included notable contributions from Heinrich Ignaz Franz Biber (1644–1704) and Johann Paul von Westhoff (1656–1705), as well as from Bach's contemporaries Johann Georg Pisendel (1687–1755) and Georg Philipp Telemann (1681–1767).[49] When Bach arrived in Weimar in 1703 for his initial, brief tenure as a minor chamber musician and servant (*Laquey*) in the ducal court,[50] he would unquestionably have encountered Westhoff, who spent his final years there. Among the most distinguished German violinists of his generation, Westhoff had published an important collection of dance suites for unaccompanied violin (Dresden, 1696), the earliest known collection of its kind.[51] Perhaps Bach's return in 1708 to Weimar – the place where he had met Westhoff – may have planted a seed for him to conceive an extended solo-violin project.

Another important catalyst for Bach composing solo-violin music may have been his contact with Pisendel, the foremost German violinist of their generation, who visited Weimar in 1709 and whom Bach almost certainly met again in Dresden in 1717. Pisendel's *Sonata à Violino Solo Senza Baßo* (c. 1716) bears a title strikingly similar to the one Bach used in the 1720 autograph of his Violin Solos: *Sei Solo à Violino senza Basso accompagnato*. Dorian Bandy describes Pisendel's penchant for nonmelodic, chordal writing played as arpeggios across two or more strings. In such passages, the left hand fingers the underlying chord progression, and the bowing provides the arpeggiated realization.[52] Example 1.2 compares such a passage with a similar technique that appears in the Prelude to Bach's Suite No. 3 over a climactic dominant pedal: As the cellist's fingering involves chordal hand shapes, the bow flutters across three strings, expressing the harmonies as broken chords. Dissonances are prepared and resolved in the continuous voice leading felt by the cellist's left hand, even though they are literally sounded as arpeggios.

Bach and the Solo Cello; or, What Is a Violoncello?

In setting out to compose six suites for unaccompanied cello, Bach took on a significant compositional challenge. Compared to the violin, the cello's larger size demands greater stretches and more irregular fingerings, posing technical constraints that would preclude the sort of dense, chordal writing found in Bach's solo-violin fugues and Ciaconna. To adapt the German solo-violin tradition or the French solo-viol tradition for the cello would call for creative solutions to surmount these technical constraints, using compositional artifice to imply polyphony that exists only in a listener's mind, without relying on extensive chordal writing to express multiple voices more literally. The difference between Bach's writing for violin and cello is illustrated by comparing his three solo-violin fugues to his solo-cello fugue in Suite No. 5. Whereas the former are rife with finger-twisting three- and four-note chords, the latter uses limited double stops (mostly involving open strings), suggesting polyphony largely through implication (see Example 1.3).

What precisely motivated Bach to compose unaccompanied cello music is unclear. Like many of Bach's "opus" collections, they may have been written to rise to a novel challenge, perhaps to illustrate compositional virtuosity by exploring the particularities, affordances, and constraints of the cello, which was only just beginning to emerge in German lands as a solo instrument.

Did Bach play the cello? What sort of instrument was called "violoncello" during Bach's lifetime? Surprisingly, both questions resist straightforward answers. Today, the term "cello" (short for "violoncello") refers to a standardized instrument, with exactly

Bach and the Solo Cello; or, What Is a Violoncello?

Example 1.2 Solo music with chordal models representing hand shapes.
a. Johann Georg Pisendel, Sonata for unaccompanied violin, Allegro.
b. Suite No. 3 in C Major, Prelude.

Example 1.3 Suite No. 5, Prelude, fugue subject as compound melody.

four strings tuned in fifths, with a body length of 75 cm, fit with an endpin to support holding the instrument between the legs. However, for Bach's contemporaries, it referred to instruments of various sizes, often with four strings but sometimes five. Whereas larger instruments were played between the legs, medium ones could be supported by a stool or else played at the shoulder with the support of a strap. The latter style, called "violoncello da spalla" (shoulder cello) or in German sources "viola di spala" (shoulder viola), was considered a form of cello playing. The modifier "da spalla" is not indicated in scores, since it referred more to a position or playing technique than to a specific kind of instrument.[53] Figures 1.1–1.7 show images contemporaneous to Bach that depict various forms of cello playing, including viola da spalla.[54]

Since the various formats of cellos were all bass instruments and were generally suitable for the same repertoire, many musicians described them as being broadly interchangeable. In a discussion of the cello from 1710, the prolific musical critic and lexicographer Johann Mattheson (1681–1764) focused primarily on viola da spalla playing:

> The distinguished *violoncello*, the *bassa viola*, and [the] *viola di spala* are small bass violins, in comparison with the larger ones with five or even six strings, on which one can play all manner of rapid passages, variations, and ornaments with less effort than on the large machines [i.e., the more unwieldy violone].

Bach and the Solo Cello; or, What Is a Violoncello?

Figure 1.1 Figure playing viola da spalla (inhabited initial "P" for "prelude"). From Giuseppe Torelli, *Concertino per camera a violin e violoncello* (Bologna, c. 1687), violoncello partbook (detail). Reproduced by permission of the Bibliothèque nationale de France.

In particular, the *viola di spala*, or *shoulder* viola, has a great effect in accompaniment, because it can cut through strongly and express the notes cleanly. A bass [line] can never be brought out more distinctly or clearly than on this instrument. It is fastened with a band to the chest and thrown, as it were, onto the right shoulder, so that nothing stops or hinders its resonance in the slightest.[55]

A 1708 instructional manuscript by Bach's cousin and friend Johann Gottfried Walther (1684–1748) asserted that the violoncello is played in a horizontal position supported by the arm. Surprisingly, he did not even mention the possibility of holding the instrument between the legs:

Violoncello, an Italian bass instrument not unlike a *viola da gamba*, is played almost like a *violin*. Namely, it is partly supported by the left hand, which [also] stops the

Cöthen, French Style, "Opus" Collections, and the Cello

Figure 1.2 Figure playing viola da spalla. From *Procession de la Fête-Dieu à Aix-en-Provence* (c. 1710–40). Screen, oil on wood (detail). Reproduced by permission of the City of Aix-en-Provence and P. Biolatto. For a full color version of this figure, please visit www.cambridge.org/9781316511770 and navigate to the Resources tab.

strings. However, owing to its weight [it is also supported] by being attached to a coat button. It is played with a bow in the right hand [and] is tuned like a *viola*.[56]

As late as 1752, Johann Joachim Quantz (1697–1773) recommended that a cello soloist have two instruments, a larger one with thicker strings, stronger bow, and coarser (black) bow hair for ensemble (*ripieno*) playing, and a smaller one with thinner strings, suitable for navigating difficult passagework in solo music.[57] Leopold Mozart (1719–87), writing in 1756, echoed Quantz's remarks about the varying sizes of cellos, mentioning that they commonly have four strings, having formerly had five. But he added a telling detail in his discussion of the viol: Writing about the etymology of "viola da gamba" (literally "leg viola"), he observes that "*nowadays* the violoncello, too, is held between the legs."[58] Evidently, he considered the preference for playing the cello between the legs to be a recent development, implying that the viola da spalla technique had formerly been a prominent style. The

Bach and the Solo Cello; or, What Is a Violoncello?

Figure 1.3 Giovanni Battista Sintes and Arnold van Westerhout, engraving labeled "Viola," after illustration by Stefano Sparigioni. From Filippo Bonanni, *Gabinetto armonico* (Rome, 1722). Reproduced by permission of the Bodleian Library.

Figure 1.4 Bernard Picart, figure playing cello (1704). Etching (detail). Reproduced by permission of the Rijksmuseum.

organist Jakob Adlung (1699–1762) – a friend of Walther's and student of another Bach cousin – simply asserted that the "*violoncello* is also called *viola di spala*."[59] In sum, these German sources

Bach and the Solo Cello; or, What Is a Violoncello?

Figure 1.5 Thomas Gainsborough, *The Rev. John Chafy Playing the Violoncello in a Landscape* (c. 1750–52). Oil on canvas (detail). Reproduced by permission of Tate Images.

show the diversity of cello instrumental types and playing styles, of which viola da spalla was an important and integral part.[60]

Viola da spalla offered the advantage that a player would use the same basic fingerings and technique for the full range of the

23

Figure 1.6 Attributed to Charles Philips, *Portrait of a Gentleman with a Violoncello* (c. 1720). Oil on canvas (detail), present whereabouts unknown. Reproduced by permission of Bridgeman Images.

violin family, from treble (violin) to bass (violoncello) – similar to consorts of recorders or viols (or, in modern contexts, to flutes, clarinets, and saxophones).[61] An accomplished player of both violin and viola, Bach would certainly have been capable of playing viola da spalla. Although there is no record of Bach playing any kind of

Bach and the Solo Cello; or, What Is a Violoncello?

Figure 1.7 Jean-Jacques Flipart, engraving of violoncello player. Frontispiece to Michel Corrette, *Méthode théorique et pratique pour apprendre en peu de tems le violoncelle dans sa perfection* (Paris, 1741) (detail). Reproduced by permission of the Bibliothèque nationale de France.

cello, his composition of virtuoso suites that draw maximum musical effect from the minimal instrumental resources of a solo cello suggest an intimate, possibly firsthand knowledge of the instrument's idioms and capabilities.[62] As son of the Eisenach town piper (*Stadtpfeifer*), Bach would have gained experience handling all sorts of instruments since childhood, having most probably been put to work at a young age assisting with the repair or restringing of instruments that passed through the family's household.[63] In adulthood, Bach amassed a large collection of instruments – for use by his family, students, and himself – that included three violas, two cellos, and a *Bassetgen* (a smaller instrument, probably with five strings, possibly synonymous with instruments called violoncello piccolo or viola pomposa).[64]

Aside from the varying sizes and formats of cellos, another perhaps surprising difference between historical and modern playing relates to the style of bowing. Among cellists who held their instruments between the knees, many of Bach's contemporaries still used an underhand bow hold that today is adopted mostly by viol players (and a growing number of Baroque cellists).[65] Linike – the cellist at Cöthen during Bach's tenure and possibly among the first to play the Cello Suites – almost certainly would have used an underhand bow hold, which had been predominant at the time he learned to play.

The "modern," overhand bow hold gained popularity first in France and England and gradually became the standard cello technique by c. 1800. This transition in bowing style was documented by British music historian Charles Burney (1726–1814). In the 1770s, Burney heard performances by two of Europe's finest cellists, Antonio Vandini (c. 1690–1778) in Padua and Markus Heinrich Graul (d. 1799) in Berlin, remarking that both cellists "hold the bow in the old-fashioned way, with the hand under it."[66] Similar comments appear in an extended description from a 1799 review of a performance by cellist Johann Georg Christoph Schetky (1737–1824).[67] These latter two musicians, among the most prominent German cellists of their time, were both within Bach's musical orbit. Born in Bach's hometown of Eisenach, Graul married into the family of a violinist and viol player who was personally acquainted with Bach, and he became a colleague of C. P. E. Bach at the Prussian court in Berlin in the 1760s. Schetky, a native of Darmstadt, was a close musical associate of Christoph Graupner (1683–1760), Bach's one-time competitor for the St. Thomas cantorate in Leipzig.[68]

Bach and the Solo Cello; or, What Is a Violoncello?

Players who use the (modern) overhand bow hold tend to prefer *down* bows (from frog to tip) where stronger strokes are needed, such as for chords and on downbeats (per the "rule of the down-bow"). However, the opposite tends to be true for those using the underhand hold, where *up* bows (from tip to frog) are the stronger stroke. Quantz remarked in 1752 that "some [cellists] move the bow as it is customary on the viola da gamba, that is, instead of a down-stroke from left to right for the principal notes, they make an up-stroke from right to left, beginning from the tip of the bow."[69] The approach to bowings for the Cello Suites, therefore, would depend considerably on the type of instrument and bow hold. Many cellists contemporary to Bach (and his sons) used the underhand hold and would therefore have had bowing habits roughly opposite to those adopted by modern cellists. A viola da spalla player would essentially play the instrument like a very large violin, using the overhand bow hold and choosing bowings accordingly. Each of these playing styles – using a large instrument between the legs (with either underhand or overhand bow hold) or playing a smaller instrument as viola da spalla – would be conducive to different ways for the bow to navigate string crossings and slurs, resulting in various tendencies for articulation and phrasing.

One might wonder precisely which variety of cello and which bowing style Bach may have had in mind for his Cello Suites, but perhaps that may be the wrong question. Given that Bach had mastered all variety of keyboard instruments – organ, harpsichord, clavichord, and so on – with many compositions playable on various kinds, Wolff argues convincingly that Bach seems to have conceived the Cello Suites "to accommodate a fluid situation without being prescriptive" as to the precise type of instrument.[70] Moreover, since the Violin Solos and Cello Suites were compiled as a two-part collection, together they offer a survey of styles and playing techniques that spans the range of the violin family, from treble to bass. This collection of music for solo violin and cello thus exemplifies C. P. E. Bach's aforementioned remark about his father's complete understanding of all string instruments. Bach's conception of this project may well explain his rationale to compose not for solo viol – the instrument favored by his patron and his friend Abel – but instead to combine elements from the French *pièces de viole* and the German solo-violin traditions into an original synthesis for the more modern cello, then a novel solo instrument in German-speaking lands and one that belongs together with the solo violin as members of the same instrumental family. A musician who could play both books of this two-part collection would surely be considered a virtuoso on string instruments. And Bach, then known primarily as an organist and composer of keyboard music, proved his complete mastery of the violin family through the remarkably original and elaborate Violin Solos and Cello Suites, whose impact on solo-string playing and composition is felt even today.

Notes

1. Christoph Wolff, *Johann Sebastian Bach: The Learned Musician*, updated ed. (New York: W. W. Norton, 2013), 187–96.
2. Hans T. David, Arthur Mendel, and Christoph Wolff, eds., *The New Bach Reader: A Life of Johann Sebastian Bach in Letters and Documents* (New York: W. W. Norton, 1998), 43, 46–48, 80, 144–51, 172–85, 189–96, and 204. See also Robert L. Marshall, "Toward a Twenty-First-Century Bach Biography," *Musical Quarterly* 84, no. 3 (Autumn 2000): 497–525.
3. Wolff, *Bach: The Learned Musician*, 199–211. Historic Carlsbad is now known as Karlovy Vary in the Czech Republic.
4. David, Mendel, and Wolff, *New Bach Reader*, 151.
5. Cited in Wolff, *Bach: The Learned Musician*, 192.
6. Some of these compositions may have been begun in Weimar. On problems of chronology, see Andrew Talle, "Courts," in *The Routledge Research Companion to Johann Sebastian Bach*, ed. Robin A. Leaver (New York: Routledge, 2017), 196–200.
7. Cited in Wolff, *Bach: The Learned Musician*, 196, translation lightly emended.
8. Bach composed roughly one ensemble or orchestral work per week while at Cöthen, according to an analysis of bookbinder receipts that evince the large body of now-lost music. See Friedrich Smend, *Bach in Köthen*, translated by John Page, edited by Stephen Daw (St. Louis: Concordia Publishing House, 1985), 34. See also Wolff, *Bach: The Learned Musician*, 200.
9. Maik Richter, *Die Hofmusik in Köthen: von den Anfängen (um 1690) bis zum Tod Fürst Leopolds von Anhalt-Köthen* (Saarbrücken: VDM Verlag, 2010), 19–20.

Bach and the Solo Cello; or, What Is a Violoncello?

10. Chelsea Bernstein, "Bach's Cello Suites and the French Bass Viol Tradition" (DMA diss., University of Maryland, 2020).
11. Pierre Rameau, *Le Maître à danser* (Paris, 1725), ix.
12. Meredith Little and Natalie Jenne, *Dance and the Music of J.S. Bach* (Bloomington: Indiana University Press, 1991), 3–15.
13. Robert L. Marshall and Traute M. Marshall, *Exploring the World of J.S. Bach: A Traveler's Guide* (Urbana: University of Illinois Press, 2016), 23. See also Hans-Joachim Schulze, "The French Influence in Bach's Instrumental Music," *Early Music* 13, no. 2 (May 1985): 181; and Gustav Fock, *Der junge Bach in Lüneburg: 1700 bis 1702* (Hamburg: Merseburger Verlag, 1950), 42–60.
14. Louis Delpech, "Les Musiciens français en Allemagne du nord (1660–1730): Questions de méthode," *Diasporas* 26 (2015): paragraphs 12–15.
15. David, Mendel, and Wolff, *New Bach Reader*, 300.
16. Karl Geiringer and Irene Geiringer, *The Bach Family: Seven Generations of Creative Genius* (Oxford: Oxford University Press, 1954), 126. For an overview of musical life, see Samantha Owens, Barbara M. Reul, and Janice B. Stockigt, eds., *Music at German Courts, 1715–1760: Changing Artistic Priorities* (Woodbridge: Boydell & Brewer, 2012). See also Talle, "Courts."
17. Adrien Fauchier-Magnan, *The Small German Courts in the Eighteenth Century*, trans. Mervyn Savill (London: Methuen, 1958), 17–41. See also Friedrich II of Prussia, *Memoires pour servir à l'histoire de la Maison de Brandebourg*, 2 vols. (Berlin, 1751), 2:328.
18. Richter, *Die Hofmusik in Köthen*, 19–23. See also Rudolf Bunge, "Johann Sebastian Bachs Kapelle zu Cöthen und deren nachgelassene Instrumente," *Bach-Jahrbuch* 2 (1905): 19.
19. Hans-Joachim Schulze, "Von Weimar nach Köthen: Risiken und Chancen eines Amtwechsels," *Cöthener Bach-Hefte* 11 (2003): 11–14.
20. Wolff, *Bach: The Learned Musician*, 191–92. See also Martin Geck, *Johann Sebastian Bach: Life and Work*, trans. John Hargraves (Orlando: Harcourt, 2006), 101–2; and Richter, *Die Hofmusik in Köthen*, 24–26.
21. Wolff, *Bach: The Learned Musician*, 194.
22. Smend, *Bach in Köthen*, 176.
23. Philipp Spitta, *Johann Sebastian Bach: His Work and Influence on the Music of Germany, 1685–1750*, 3 vols., trans. Clara Bell and J. A. Fuller Maitland (London, 1899), 2:100.
24. Jean Rousseau, *Traité de la viole* (Paris, 1687), 56–64.
25. Sieur de Machy, *Pièces de violle* (Paris, 1685), 7.
26. On the more intimate musical activities that would have taken place in Leopold's private quarters – as opposed to the larger, more formal Hall of Mirrors (*Spiegelsaal*) – see Smend, *Bach in Köthen*, 174–76.

27. For an overview of the solo viol tradition in France, see Shaun Kam Fook Ng, "Le Sieur de Machy and the French Solo Viol Tradition" (MA thesis, University of Western Australia, 2008), 14–66. On its influence in Germany, see Bernstein, "Bach's Cello Suites," 40–97 and 153–258. See also David Ledbetter, *Unaccompanied Bach: Performing the Solo Works* (New Haven: Yale University Press, 2009), 35–46; and Clemens Fanselau, *Mehrstimmigkeit in J. S. Bachs Werken für Melodieinstrumente ohne Begleitung* (Berlin: Schewe, 2000), 29–34.
28. Kai Köpp, "Vom Ensemble- zum Soloinstrument: Das Violoncello," in *Bachs Orchester- und Kammermusik: Das Handbuch*, 2 vols., ed. Siegbert Rampe (Laaber: Laaber Verlag, 2013), 2:253–63.
29. On the changing fortunes of the viol and the cello, see Hubert Le Blanc, *Défense de la basse de viole contre les entréprises du violon et les prétentions du violoncel* (Amsterdam, 1740).
30. Brent Wissick, "The Cello Music of Antonio Bononcini: Violone, Violoncello da Spalla, and the Cello 'Schools' of Bologna and Rome," *Journal of Seventeenth-Century Music* 12, no. 2 (2006), www.sscm-jscm.org/v12/no1/wissick.html. See also Mark Chambers, "The 'Mistuned' Cello: Precursors to J. S. Bach's Suite V in C Minor for Unaccompanied Violoncello" (DMA diss., Florida State University, 1996), 25–41.
31. Christoph Wolff, *Bach's Musical Universe: The Composer and His Work* (New York: W. W. Norton, 2020), 20–22. See also Elaine Sisman, "Six of One: The Opus Concept in the Eighteenth Century," in *The Century of Bach and Mozart: Perspectives on Historiography, Composition, Theory, and Performance*, ed. Thomas Forrest Kelly and Sean Gallagher (Cambridge, MA: Harvard University Press), 79–107.
32. David, Mendel, and Wolff, *New Bach Reader*, 304.
33. For an analysis of the obituary's works list, see Wolff, *Bach's Musical Universe*, 13–25.
34. David, Mendel, and Wolff, *New Bach Reader*, 397.
35. Wolff, *Bach: The Learned Musician*, 42–43.
36. David, Mendel, and Wolff, *New Bach Reader*, 472.
37. David, Mendel, and Wolff, *New Bach Reader*, 472.
38. Ledbetter, *Unaccompanied Bach*, 10–11.
39. Wolff, *Bach's Musical Universe*, 87.
40. Andrew Talle, "Some Observations on the Sources for Bach's *Violin Soli* and *Cello Suites*," *BACH* 53, no. 1 (2022): 4.
41. On Bach's elaborate audition recital in Hamburg, see David, Mendel, and Wolff, *New Bach Reader*, 89–91; and Wolff, *Bach: The Learned Musician*, 211–15.

42. Personal communication with Christoph Wolff, email dated November 20, 2022. See also Wolff, *Bach's Musical Universe*, 88–89.
43. Wolff, *Bach's Musical Universe*, 88.
44. Bettina Schwemer and Douglas Woodfull-Harris, eds., *6 Suites a Violoncello Solo senza Basso, BWV 1007–1012*, by J. S. Bach (Kassel: Bärenreiter, 2000), text volume, 9.
45. Andrew Talle, revised preface to *Six Suites for Violoncello Solo, BWV 1007–1012*, by J. S. Bach, ed. Andrew Talle (Kassel: Bärenreiter, 2018; 3rd rev. printing, 2022), xxxv.
46. David Schulenberg, *The Keyboard Music of J.S. Bach*, 2nd ed. (New York: Routledge, 2006), 38 and 278.
47. On the key schemes of the Violin Solos and Cello Suites, see Ledbetter, *Unaccompanied Bach*, 11.
48. Wolff, *Bach's Musical Universe*, 67. On the division of Bach's career between the early organ-focused and the more varied roles in Cöthen and Leipzig, see also Wolff, *Bach: The Learned Musician*, 187–88.
49. For an overview of music for solo violin or flute composed near Weimar and Cöthen during Bach's lifetime, see Fanselau, *Mehrstimmigkeit*, 65–69.
50. Wolff, *Bach: The Learned Musician*, 68. See also Wolff, *Bach's Musical Universe*, 86; and Talle, "Courts," 195.
51. Johann Paul von Westhoff's 1696 suites publication may be a second volume or a reprinting of an earlier set (now lost) published in Dresden in 1682. See Folker Göthel and Peter Wollny, "Westhoff, Johann Paul von," in *Grove Music Online*, ed. Deane Root (published January 20, 2001).
52. Dorian Bandy, "Violin Technique and the Contrapuntal Imagination in 17th-Century German Lands," *Early Music* 49, no. 2 (May 2021): 285.
53. Gregory Barnett, "The Violoncello da Spalla: Shouldering the Cello in the Baroque Era," *Journal of the American Musical Instrument Society* 24 (1998): 103. See also Dmitry Badiarov, "The Violoncello, Viola da Spalla and Viola Pomposa in Theory and Practice," *The Galpin Society Journal* 60 (April 2007): 140.
54. For additional illustrations of historical cello playing, see Barnett, "The Violoncello da Spalla," 90–104; Badiarov, "The Violoncello," 134–45; Köpp, "Vom Ensemble- zum Soloinstrument"; B. E. Tinbergen, "The 'Cello' in the Low Countries: The Instrument and Its Practical Use in the 17th and 18th Centuries" (PhD diss., Leiden University, 2018); Marc Vanscheeuwijck, "Recent Re-evaluations of the Baroque Cello and What They Might Mean for Performing the Music of J. S. Bach," *Early Music* 48, no. 2 (May 2010): 181–92; and Vanscheeuwijck, "The Baroque Cello and Its Performance," *Performance Practice Review* 9, no. 1 (Spring 1996): 78–96.

55. Johann Mattheson, *Das neu-eröffnete Orchestre* (Hamburg, 1713), 285. This definition is repeated, nearly verbatim, in the following two sources: Joseph Friedrich Bernhard Caspar Majer, *Neu-eröffnete theoretisch und pracktischer Music-Saal* (Nuremberg, 1741), 99; and Johann Gottfried Walther, *Musicalisches Lexikon* (Leipzig, 1732), 637. See also Johann Philipp Eisel, *Musicus Autodidaktos* (Erfurt, 1738), 44–46.
56. Johann Gottfried Walther, *Praecepta der musicalischen Composition*, ed. Peter Benary (Leipzig: Breitkopf & Härtel, 1955), 56.
57. Johann Joachim Quantz, *On Playing the Flute*, trans. Edward R. Reilly (London: Faber & Faber, 1985), 241.
58. Leopold Mozart, *A Treatise on the Fundamental Principles of Violin Playing*, 2nd ed., trans. Editha Knocker (Oxford: Oxford University Press, 1951), 11; emphasis added.
59. Jakob Adlung, *Anleitung zu der musikalischen Gelahrtheit* (Erfurt, 1758), 599.
60. On the viola da spalla in Northern Italy, see Barnett, "The Violoncello da Spalla," 81–90; and Alessandro Sanguineti, "Da Spalla or Da Gamba? The Early Cello in Northern Italian Repertoire, 1650–95," *Galpin Society Journal* 69 (April 2016): 99–108.
61. Barnett, "The Violoncello da Spalla," 100.
62. For speculation about Bach as cellist, see Spitta, *Johann Sebastian Bach*, 2:69–70; and Wolff, *Bach's Musical Universe*, 67–68.
63. Wolff, *Bach: The Learned Musician*, 22–23.
64. David, Mendel, and Wolff, *New Bach Reader*, 252. On terminological problems related to viola pomposa and violoncello piccolo, see Badiarov, "The Violoncello."
65. Mark Smith, "The Cello Bow Held the Viol-Way: Once Common, but Now Almost Forgotten," *Chelys: The Journal of the Viola da Gamba Society* 24 (1995): 47–60. On iconographic evidence of this bow hold, see Tinbergen, "The 'Cello' in the Low Countries," 112–24.
66. Quoted in Smith, "The Cello Bow," 50. Vandini's underhand bow hold was also documented in Christoph Gottlieb von Murr, *Journal zur Kunstgeschichte und zur allgemeinen Litteratur, Zweyter Theil* (Nuremberg, 1776), 23. For a drawing of Vandini's bow hold, see Vanscheeuwijck, "Recent Re-evaluations," 184.
67. Smith, "The Cello Bow," 50–53.
68. Talle, revised preface, xxxv–xxxvi.
69. Quantz, *On Playing the Flute*, 241.
70. Wolff, *Bach's Musical Universe*, 96.

2

DANCE TYPES, PRELUDES, AND ANALYTICAL PERSPECTIVES

This chapter offers an overview of the types of preludes and dances included in Bach's Cello Suites, as well as of analytical approaches that reveal how a suite hangs together as a unified whole. Bach's instrumental suites were not composed as functional dances. Indeed, the dance types commonly included in German suites had to varying degrees developed into stylized instrumental genres by Bach's lifetime. Some retained a close connection to ballroom or ballet music, while others (such as allemandes) had grown more abstract and bore a more remote relationship to their dance origins.

Although the most extensive sources on *la belle danse* are French, the present survey will emphasize Bach's North German contemporaries, especially Walther and Mattheson. Their descriptions of the various dances give a sense of how musicians in Bach's orbit understood the instrumental suite and suggest ways each dance type could be characterized in performance. Bach's conceptions of dance genres surely came mainly from repertoire rather than theoretical texts, but he nevertheless owned and must have consulted various musical books, including Walther's *Musicalisches Lexikon*, for which he served as a sales representative.[1]

As a complement to reading theoretical descriptions of dance types, the best way to get to know them is to play through (or listen to) many examples by Bach and his contemporaries. Bach required his keyboard students to play "a number of suites" as a bridge between studying his *Inventions* and the *Well-Tempered Clavier*.[2] Bach's student Johann Philipp Kirnberger (1721–83) recommended that a musician should "diligently play all sorts of characteristic dances ... [in order to become] accustomed to distinguishing the rhythm of each one ... [and] to give each piece its own expression, because each of these dance types [*Tanzmelodien*] has its own characteristic meter and note values."[3] Bach's

33

Dance Types, Preludes, and Analytical Perspectives

biographer Forkel also remarked on rhythm in relation to the characters of dance types within Baroque suites:

In these suites were, between preludes and the concluding jigs, many French characteristic pieces and dance tunes, in which the rhythm was the most important object. The composers were therefore obliged to make use of a great variety of time, measure, and rhythm. Bach carried this branch of the art also much farther than any of his predecessors or contemporaries.[4]

Allemande

Named for the French word meaning "German," the allemande is the first of the core suite movements. Walther described the allemande as "serious and grave,"[5] whereas Mattheson remarked that it expresses "a content or satisfied spirit, which enjoys good order and calm."[6] Like all of Bach's dance movements, the allemande is divided into two repeated sections called "reprises." Composed in a duple meter (typically notated as ₵, less often ¢), its two reprises each begin with a short upbeat, often a single eighth or sixteenth note but sometimes three notes (as in Suite No. 3).

Another characteristic of many allemandes is the use of a double cadence at the end of each reprise. By "double cadence," I mean that the downbeat of a reprise's final measure marks the arrival from dominant to tonic, followed immediately by a measure-long flourish embellishing that cadential tonic chord, arriving at the end of the bar on a bass note or chord that reasserts that same harmony (see Example 2.1). Double cadences are found in Allemandes from Suite No. 1 (mm. 16 and 32), Suite No. 2 (mm. 12 and 24), Suite No. 3 (mm. 12 and 24), Suite No. 5 (mm. 18 and 36), and Suite No. 6 (mm. 8 and 20).

Among the dances included in Bach's Cello Suites, the allemandes are the most abstract and stylistically variable. The Allemande of Suite No. 5, with its *alla breve* meter (¢) and dotted rhythms, evokes the French theatrical style and invites an over-dotted performance, whereas the florid Allemande from Suite No. 6, written mostly in melismatic thirty-second notes under long slurs, is like a written-out improvisation somewhat comparable to the opening movements of the Solo Violin Sonatas Nos. 1

Courante

Example 2.1 Suite No. 3 in C Major, Allemande, double cadence.

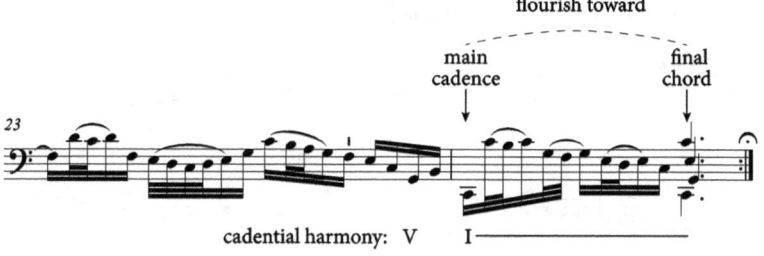

and 2. The Allemandes of Suites Nos. 5–6 contrast sharply with the more typical examples in all other suites, which employ mostly eighth and sixteenth notes and shorter slurs. This variability reflects that the allemande had become a stylized musical genre that was no longer used for ballroom dancing. Both Mattheson and Walther described it as a category of instrumental piece, without even mentioning its origins as a German dance.[7] Even a century earlier, the French polymath Marin Mersenne (1588–1648) had already considered the allemande to have fallen out of favor as dance music: "The *allemande* is a dance from Germany ... [that] is today played on instruments without dancing ... unless it is in a ballet."[8]

Courante

The term "courante" derives from a French word primarily meaning "running" but with other related meanings, including flowing water (*eau courante*), as in the current of a stream or river. The Leipzig dance master Gottfried Tauber (1670–1746) invoked this sense of flowing water, writing that "a good courante dancer swims, so to speak, and, as a swift stream of water, shoots away very quickly."[9] Characterized by its "running, lively melody,"[10] according to Mattheson, the courante expresses "sweet hopefulness," since "there is something of the hearty, something of longing and also something of the cheerful in this melody: only those things from which hope is composed."[11] Kirnberger contrasted the "lively and light" Italian corrente with the "serious, solid character" of the courante in France and Germany.[12]

Dance Types, Preludes, and Analytical Perspectives

Example 2.2 Suite No. 5 in C Minor, Courante, hemiola effects.

The courantes in Bach's Cello Suites begin with short upbeats, usually an eighth note. All but one are notated in $\frac{3}{4}$ and make extensive use of sixteenth notes, features that indicate the influence of the virtuoso, Italianate corrente, despite Bach's use of the French form of the title. The Courante from Suite No. 2, for example, is a driving movement with running sixteenths almost throughout. That movement resembles the *moto perpetuo* double of the Corrente from the Solo Violin Partita No. 1 and the quasi–*moto perpetuo* Correntes from the Keyboard Partita No. 3 (BWV827) and the Solo Flute Partita (BWV1013).

The only true French courante among the Cello Suites is that of Suite No. 5, which alone uses the traditionally French $\frac{3}{2}$ meter. Many French courantes feature hemiola effects, whereby a meter initially counted as **1–2–3|1–2–3** later becomes **1–2–3|1-2-3** (i.e., a slower count, with three half-note beats spread over two measures); see, for example, the Courante from the English Suite No. 3 (BWV808). A related metrical feature often appears in the final bars of each reprise, where $\frac{3}{2}$ suddenly sounds like $\frac{6}{4}$ (i.e., effectively two fast three-counts per bar, instead of one slower one). In the English Suites, all courantes are notated in $\frac{3}{2}$ and feature this $\frac{6}{4}$ effect in the final measure of each reprise. These types of metrical manipulation figure prominently in the Courante from Suite No. 5 (see Example 2.2).

Sarabande

Originating as a sung dance in Latin America and popularized in Spain, where it was banned in 1583 for its erotic, lascivious nature, the sarabande by Bach's lifetime had long since been reinvented as a slower, noble dance. Walther described its "grave" character,[13] and Matteson held that the sarabande expresses "ambition," adding that sarabandes intended for dancing should avoid running notes, which would undermine their "grandeur" and "seriousness."[14] Bach's sarabandes are mostly notated in $\frac{3}{4}$. Those few sarabandes written in $\frac{3}{2}$, as in Suite No. 6, invite a slower performance tempo.[15]

The notion that sarabandes are characterized by an emphasized or elongated second beat is valid but calls for some nuance. Some (not all) sarabandes tend to place emphasis on the second beats of many bars. Such emphasis is often expressed with a basic rhythm of ♩ ♩ (or ♩ 𝅗𝅥 for sarabandes in $\frac{3}{2}$), placing long notes and/or long harmonies on the second beats. Such "long notes" on second beats are often obscured by ornamental notes that decorate an underlying short-long basic rhythm. Example 2.3 shows how harmonic rhythm (rate of harmonic change) tends to reinforce the basic ♩ ♩ rhythm. In the Sarabande from Suite No. 3, dissonant suspensions on the second beats also confer some emphasis.

In the Sarabande from Suite No. 5 (shown in Example 2.3c), the slurring pattern tends to suggest an underlying rhythm of ♩ ♩, an apparent exception to the tendency to emphasize the second beats. Yet the unusual, mid-slur appoggiatura dissonances falling

Example 2.3 Sarabandes, emphasis on second beats.
  a. Suite No. 1 in G Major.
  b. Suite No. 3 in C Major.
  c. Suite No. 5 in C Minor.

on the second beats of many measures tend to confer a subtle emphasis. That emphasis is intensified in measures where the second beat is approached by the "harsh" leap of a diminished fourth.[16]

Menuet

"*Menuets* are probably known by everyone," wrote Mattheson.[17] Surely the best known of the galanteries, menuets have long been used for instruction in performance and composition, as in the familiar examples from the *Little Notebook for Anna Magdalena*

Bourrée

Example 2.4 Suite No. 1, Menuet I, two-bar units (*pas de menuet*).

Bach.[18] Named for its "nimble and small steps," from a French word meaning "small,"[19] the menuet in Mattheson's description expresses "moderate cheerfulness."[20]

Since the menuet remained a popular dance during Bach's lifetime, his menuets closely resemble functional dance music.[21] Specifically, although the menuet is notated in $\frac{3}{4}$, the dance is counted in six, with one *pas de menuet* corresponding to two measures. For this reason, Bach's menuets tend to be composed in two-bar units, with "resting points" or cadences falling every four or eight measures (see Example 2.4).

Bourrée

Originally a French country dance, the bourrée had become popular in ballrooms by around 1700. A duple-meter courtship dance, it is characterized by Mattheson as conveying "contentment and pleasantness ... as if it were untroubled or calm, a little slow, [and] easygoing."[22] He further described it as "solid, strong, weighty, and yet soft or delicate" and "more suited for shoving, sliding, or gliding than lifting, hopping, or springing."[23] Mattheson's commentary evokes a vivid kinesthetic image suggesting a much calmer tempo and more relaxed character than is typical in today's performances.

Bach's bourrées are usually notated with a meter of ¢ and begin with an upbeat, most often two eighth notes or a single quarter. As

Example 2.5 Suite No. 3 in C Major, Bourrées I and II, "dactylic" rhythm.

in Suite No. 3, Bach's bourrées usually feature the rhythm ♩ ♫, which Walther characterizes as "dactylic" (see Example 2.5).[24]

Gavotte

Well after the gavotte was established as a French courtly dance, it nevertheless retained some pastoral associations reflecting its folk origins.[25] For instance, in Bach's Suite No. 6, the harmonically rich Gavotte I contrasts with the simpler Gavotte II, whose rustic character is revealed most fully in an extended passage over an open D-string drone (mm. 12–20). Similar musette-like drones are found in the Gavotte II movements from the English Suites Nos. 3 and 6 (BWV808 and BWV811).

Mattheson wrote that the gavotte expresses "jubilation," adding that "the skipping nature is a true trait of these gavottes; not the running."[26] Such "skipping" accords with Bach's typical gavotte rhythms: Notated with a meter of ₵ (or sometimes 2, which was the French equivalent),[27] Bach's gavottes begin with an upbeat of two quarter notes and tend to proceed with a mixture of half and quarter notes, with occasional eighths.

A characteristic feature of Bach's gavottes is a phrase organization with "resting points" or cadences on the downbeats of even-numbered bars. The pianist Edward Aldwell (1938–2006) encouraged his students to feel this organization by counting gavottes 2–3–4–1, 2–3–4–1 (as in Example 2.6).[28] That method encourages hearing the gavotte's phrases as extended upbeats oriented toward arrivals ("1") on downbeats of even-numbered bars.

Gigue

Example 2.6 Suite No. 6 in D Major, Gavottes I and II, phrase counting after Edward Aldwell.
  a. Gavotte I.
  b. Gavotte II.

Gigue

Serving as a suite's lively finale, the courtly French gigue apparently originated in the jig of the British Isles, a term that may originate in words for fiddles (similar to the German "Geige") or possibly the (archaic) French verb "giguer," meaning "to frolic, leap, or gambol." Mattheson wrote of "ardent and fleeting zeal" and "extreme *speed* or *volatility*."[29] Bach's gigues are notated variously in $\frac{3}{8}$, $\frac{6}{8}$, and $\frac{12}{8}$. A gigue in $\frac{3}{8}$ might tend to invite a somewhat weightier, possibly slower performance than one in $\frac{12}{8}$. Whereas Bach's keyboard gigues often feature imitative polyphony, his gigues for solo violin and cello generate excitement through other means such as virtuoso display.

The brilliant style of the Gigues from Suites Nos. 4 and 6 suggest the Italian form of the dance, known as "giga" (see Example 2.7). The opposite stylistic extreme is found in the Gigue from Suite No. 5, the only true French gigue among the Cello Suites (compare to the Gigue from the French Suite No. 2, BWV813). An elegant movement in its restraint, its nearly constant use of the ♩.♪♩ rhythmic figure is such that the most prominent event in each reprise is a moment of reprieve when freer rhythms appear to mark modulations that prepare each reprise-ending cadence (mm. 15–20 near the cadence in E♭ and mm. 61–66 near the final cadence in C minor).

Example 2.7 Two styles of gigues.
a. Suite No. 6 in D Major: Italian giga (brilliant style).
b. Suite No. 5 in C Minor: French gigue.

Composing a Suite: Elements of Cyclic Unity

I will *now* set you a *Sett*, or a *Suit of Lessons* (as we commonly call *Them*) which may be of any *Number*, as you please, yet commonly are about *Half a Dozen*.

The First always, should begin in the Nature of a *Voluntary Play*, which we call a *Prœludium*, or *Prœlude*.

Then, *Allmaine, Ayre, Coranto, Seraband, Toy*, or what you please, provided They be all in the *same Key*; yet (in my opinion) in regard we call Them a *Suit of Lessons*[.] They ought to be something a Kin (as we use to say) or to have some kind of *Resemblance in their Conceits, Natures, or Humours*.[30]

Composing a Suite: Elements of Cyclic Unity

Possibly the earliest definition of the instrumental suite as a set form, this description by the English lutenist Thomas Mace (c. 1612–1706) would apply reasonably well to Bach's instrumental suites. But what of his requirement for kinship or resemblance among the movements of a suite? Another expression of the same principle comes from North German organist Martin Heinrich Fuhrmann (1669–1745), who wrote in 1706 that an allemande "is like the proposition in a musical suite, from which the corrente, sarabande, and gigue flow as parts."[31] Fuhrmann's commentary evokes a rhetorical simile, as the assertion of an argument (*propositio*) and its division into parts (*partitio*) are traditional components of a classical oration. His remarks are transmitted nearly verbatim by Walther.[32] Both Fuhrmann and Walther seem to be thinking of suites without preludes – such as Bach's French Suites – where the allemande stands as the opening movement.

The most elaborate discussion of this theme is in a 1706 treatise on variation by Friedrich Erhard Niedt (1674–1708) that illustrates a compositional method to achieve unity throughout the movements of a keyboard suite.[33] Taking a simple figured-bass progression as a starting point, Niedt applies various keyboard figurations and textures to realize it as a prelude. He then adapts the same underlying figured-bass model into meters appropriate for each movement of a dance suite (e.g., ¢ allemande, 3 or $\frac{6}{4}$ for courante, etc.), realizing the progression with a variety of rhythms and melodic figurations suitable for each dance type.[34] In this way, he generates a variation suite, where the shared figured-bass progression assures a "family resemblance" among the various movements.[35] Niedt was a student of Bach's cousin Johann Nicolaus, and Bach may have used at least the first volume of Niedt's treatise in his teaching.[36]

Bach's Cello Suites have hints of the cyclic unity described by Fuhrmann, Walther, and Niedt. In Suite No. 1, the Prelude introduces a harmonic paradigm (mm. 1–4) that returns in varied forms in the openings of the Sarabande and Menuet I (see Example 2.8).[37] Although these passages look different on the page, cellists tend to use similar fingerings for each, enabling the harmonic paradigm to be felt in the left hand. A related unifying element is the specific voicing of the tonic chord that opens the

43

Dance Types, Preludes, and Analytical Perspectives

Example 2.8 Suite No. 1 in G Major, harmonic motive.

suite – G–d–b, with two open strings – which returns prominently to open each movement, either as a block chord (Allemande in m. 1, Sarabande in mm. 1–2, Gigue in m. 4) or in arpeggiated form (Courante in mm. 1–2, Menuet I in mm. 1 and 4, and Menuet II in a minor-mode version). That chord voicing arises almost inevitably out of the affordances of the cello's open strings, but it nevertheless becomes a characteristic sonority.[38]

The Prelude to Suite No. 3 opens with an idea so simple as to seem almost generic: A descending C major scale and arpeggio, in running notes, connects c' to C, precipitously traversing the space from the cello's upper register to its lowest note, the resonant C string, which is emphasized as the first long note. Variations on this figure (shown in Example 2.9) return to open the Allemande (m. 1) and Courante (mm. 1–2). More abstractly, a descending C major scale can also be traced in the first phrase of the Bourrée I.

Composing a Suite: Elements of Cyclic Unity

Example 2.9 Suite No. 3 in C Major, c' to C scalar motive.

Finally, the Gigue's energetic opening inverts the figure, with a triumphant, ascending scale from c (m. 1) to c' (m. 3).[39]

In the Prelude to Suite No. 4, the opening harmonic gesture transforms the initial E♭ tonic harmony (mm. 1–2) into a dominant-seventh chord by adding d♭' (mm. 3–4). Two other movements likewise introduce a prominent, early melodic emphasis on d♭' as a chordal seventh and as the first chromatic pitch: the Allemande (m. 3) and the Sarabande (m. 1). Such harmonic "callbacks" give the impression of a later movement expounding upon ideas from the Prelude or revisiting unfinished business (see Example 2.10).

In Suite No. 2, a shared emphasis on the Neapolitan harmony (E♭ major) unites the first and last movements (see Example 2.11). The final section of the Prelude is preoccupied with a motive E♭–D–C♯, stated first in a middle register (mm. 49–50), then in the cello's lowest register (mm. 53–54), and finally in an intense statement in the highest register (mm. 58–59), ushering in the Prelude's closing chords. A focus on the note E♭ returns in the Gigue, first subtly (m. 11) and then more insistently toward the end (mm. 69–72).

These examples show that several Cello Suites are held together by musical ideas introduced in their preludes that are developed in later movements.[40] But even where such cyclical elements may be difficult to identify, every suite adheres to the most basic unity, namely, that all movements are in the same key. For Suites

Example 2.10 Suite No. 4 in E♭ Major, emphasis on D♭.

Example 2.11 Suite No. 2 in D Minor, emphasis on Neapolitan harmony (E♭ major).

Nos. 5–6 – composed, respectively, for *scordatura* cello and five-string cello – the same tuning and number of strings are, of course, used throughout. The "feel" of the cello in a particular key (and tuning) contributes to each suite's distinctive sound and character. Suite No. 1 emphasizes all four of the cello's open strings (especially in the Prelude), like an introduction to the instrument in its most "natural" form. In Suite No. 6, the addition of a fifth string expands the cello's upper range, facilitating that suite's brilliant style and expansive scope. Suites Nos. 3 (in C major) and 5 (in C minor) both exploit the resonance of the cello's low C string. Suite No. 5 is further characterized by novel sonorities afforded by its *scordatura* tuning – such as the chord g–d′–g′ played with three open strings – and by the French stylistic elements throughout the

suite. Finally, Suite No. 4 (in E♭ major) is the only one whose tonic and dominant notes are not open strings, which likewise gives the cello a distinctive sound (and poses intonational challenges). In sum, each suite has its own "flavor," fostered by the sound of the cello in a particular key and, in many cases, by unifying material that returns across the movements.

Preludes and Preluding

Since the core movements of a suite commence with its allemande, a prelude is in some sense before the suite's proper beginning, as suggested by its Latin etymology: *prae-* ("before") plus *ludere* ("to play"). A prelude is essentially a written-out improvisation, a composition that emulates a musician testing out their instrument and their musical ideas as preparation for the music to follow. The historical German verbs meaning "to prelude" (*präludiren*) and "to fantasize" (*fantasiren*) both emphasize the conception of the prelude and fantasia as extemporized genres. Even when composed in advance, many preludes can be played with such freedom as to simulate or reenact their improvisation.

C. P. E. Bach's treatise on keyboard playing culminates in a chapter on the improvisation of fantasias and preludes:

There are occasions when an accompanist must extemporize before the beginning of a piece. Because such an improvisation is to be regarded as a prelude which prepares the listener for the content of the piece that follows, it is more restricted than the fantasia. ... The construction of the former is determined by the nature of the piece which it prefaces; and the content or affect of this piece becomes the material out of which the prelude is fashioned.[41]

These remarks recall Fuhrmann's idea that an opening movement – for Fuhrmann an allemande, but for C. P. E. Bach a prelude – should introduce the main ideas of and accord with the style of the music to follow. He continues to outline some specific principles and methods for the improvisation of preludes, including

(1) that the principal key should be well established at the outset and confirmed at the close, often with tonic pedal points;
(2) that the middle of a prelude should modulate to a few closely related keys (and avoid more remote keys);

(3) that a natural means to achieve such modulations is by harmonizing scalar bass lines;
(4) that such modulations will introduce the leading tone of the new keys (and may or may not lead to cadences in new keys); and
(5) that a dominant pedal is an effective means to prepare for the final return to the tonic.[42]

The methods outlined by C. P. E. Bach shed light on the design of his father's preludes and allow us to imagine how they were improvised or composed.[43]

Setting aside the Prelude to Suite No. 5 – an exceptional case composed in the style of a French *ouverture* – the remaining five Cello Suite preludes can be divided into two basic categories: (modified) pattern preludes and through-composed preludes. Bach's best-known pattern prelude is the Prelude in C Major from the *Well-Tempered Clavier*, book 1, in which a single figuration obtains throughout. The Preludes to Cello Suites Nos. 1 and 4 follow a similar procedure, with a pattern established at the outset that continues throughout much of each piece. However, they would best be described as *modified* pattern preludes, since the regularity of the pattern is occasionally interrupted by cadenza-like passages (as in the Prelude in C Minor from the *Well-Tempered Clavier*, book 1). If the pattern represents the "normal" measures, the cadenza-like passages stand apart, suggesting a breakdown of the established order and a search for a return to regularity. In the Suite No. 1 Prelude (shown in Example 2.12), the figuration of the first section contrasts with the freer scales (mm. 29–30) and *bariolage* figuration (alternating notes on adjacent strings) emphasizing the open A and D strings (mm. 31–38), preparing for a climactic return of the original pattern (mm. 39–42).

A looser design is found in the through-composed Preludes to Suites Nos. 2, 3, and 6. Those preludes establish a head motive at the outset that returns to mark significant arrivals in new keys, somewhat in the manner of a ritornello. Connecting these junctures is free material with varied rhythms and figurations, often using sequences that facilitate modulations. Regardless of the style of prelude – modified pattern or through-composed – the basic procedures outlined by C. P. E. Bach broadly apply. A

Analysis of Suite No. 4

Example 2.12 Suite No. 1 in G Major, Prelude, modified pattern prelude.
 a. Opening pattern.
 b. Freer material.

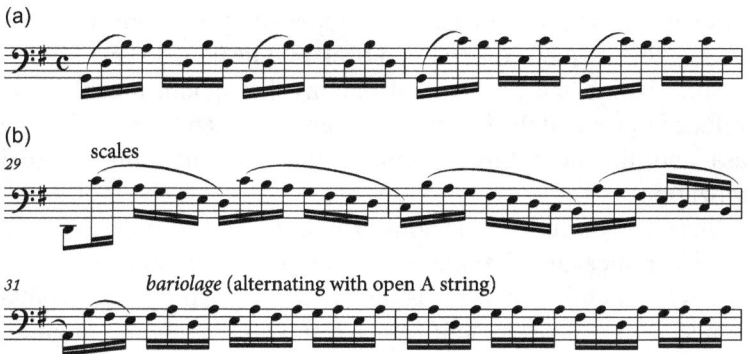

prelude begins by establishing its main key, sometimes with a tonic pedal or another chord progression emphasizing tonic. After modulating to a few closely related keys, often by means of scalar bass lines and/or sequential figuration, a prelude tends to achieve a climax with emphasis on the dominant (often a dominant pedal) followed by a final resolution to the tonic. The tonal return is sometimes emphasized with a coda that may include a tonic pedal.

Analysis of Suite No. 4

The remainder of this chapter is devoted to Suite No. 4, which poses particular technical and musical challenges. The ensuing analysis illustrates how the suite's Prelude traces an arc from the regularity of its opening pattern through a wild breakdown of musical order, leading finally through a fraught path to restore the musical equilibrium. That arc is rich with implications for how the Prelude might be shaped and characterized in performance. The suite's dance movements all follow a basic plan involving three main cadences that serve as key arrivals outlining their form. Readers are encouraged to have an *Urtext* score (with measure numbers) at hand.

Dance Types, Preludes, and Analytical Perspectives

Prelude

Whereas C. P. E. Bach's and Niedt's methods of improvising preludes begin with a figured-bass model that is fleshed out into a prelude, Example 2.13 adopts an opposite procedure by transforming the finished composition back into its figured-bass model. In Suite No. 4, the pattern that obtains throughout much of the Prelude is such that the first note of each figure can be treated as the bass and the next three notes as the corresponding chordal realization.

Since the Prelude's harmonic rhythm is slow, with just one chord per measure, Example 2.13 offers a "zoomed out" perspective, whereby each measure in the original score is transformed into a quarter note. As a result, the Prelude's regular, four-bar units are represented in the example as single measures.[44] Example 2.13 is *both* an abstract representation of the Prelude from a "bird's eye" perspective *and* a piece one can play through that sounds in many respects like the original piece. If performances of this Prelude sometimes suffer from a certain heaviness arising from a performed emphasis on most every downbeat – a habit that arises partly from the technical challenge of crossing from the cello's lowest string to its highest at the beginning of each bar – playing through Example 2.13 offers a new way to experience the harmonic flow of the Prelude's phrases.

Following the opening tonic pedal (mm. 1–9), the bass line begins a sequential passage composed of descending scale fragments. That passage hints briefly at B♭ major (mm. 13–15) and A♭ major (mm. 17–19) before achieving a stronger cadence in C minor (mm. 21–28), emphasizing the cello's resonant C string. That arrival is marked by a C minor chord that lasts two measures (mm. 27–28), the first two-measure-long harmony since the opening of the Prelude. No sooner is C minor achieved than it is destabilized, with a C dominant-seventh chord in the unstable $^4_2$ position (mm. 29–30). After a fleeting return to E♭ major (mm. 37–39), the Prelude begins a long and fraught path toward G minor. The telltale signs of a trajectory toward G minor are the F♯s beginning in m. 41 and the bass's descending natural-minor scale fragment g–f–e♭–d in mm. 45–48.

Analysis of Suite No. 4

Example 2.13 Suite No. 4 in E♭ Major, Prelude, figured-bass reduction.

When that bass scale arrives on C♯ (the fermata in m. 49), the Prelude is poised to efficiently reach a cadence in G minor (such as with a hypothetical bass line of C♯–D–G). While a G minor cadence does eventually come to fruition, it is anything but efficient: The C♯ fermata in m. 49, implying an intense, fully diminished-seventh chord, effects an abrupt breakdown of the Prelude's pattern of figuration. A series of freewheeling cadenzas ensues (beginning in m. 49), including an abortive attempt to restore the Prelude's pattern (mm. 52–55). The section emphasizing the dominant of G minor includes a severe dominant-ninth chord (m. 59) and an "effortful" passage of three- and four-note chords (mm. 59–61) before the Prelude finally achieves the hard-won cadence in G minor (m. 62).

Marking the end of a troubled episode, the G minor cadence coincides with the restoration of the Prelude's pattern, seemingly for good. Moving through a scalar bass line (G–A♭–A♮–B♭ in mm. 62–70), the Prelude arrives at a dominant pedal (mm. 70–81), marked once again by freer, cadenza-like figuration and a pass through the evocative Neapolitan harmony (mm. 80–81) before achieving the structural V–I cadence in m. 82. What follows is a coda on a tonic pedal that counterbalances the harmonic turmoil of the Prelude's middle section. The coda essentially reenacts the Prelude's opening (compare mm. 82–87 to mm. 1–6), with a florid cadenza decorating the affirmative final cadence.

The foregoing analysis mostly demonstrates the alignment between Example 2.13 and C. P. E. Bach's approach to improvising preludes. What follows adds a more subjective layer that interprets the Prelude through Christian symbolism, with special attention to the musical "crisis" brought about by the C♯ fermata in m. 49. This discussion is inspired by an imaginative analytical essay by Carl Schachter.[45] Although there is little evidence to suggest that Bach read hidden religious meanings into secular dance music, Schachter's interpretation nevertheless offers a metaphorical "story" of the Prelude's musical events that some musicians may find illuminating.[46]

The Prelude's basic pattern of figuration (as in m. 1) comprises a bass note (E♭) plus a three-note descending arpeggio (e′♭–b♭–g).

Analysis of Suite No. 4

Example 2.14 *Niederfallen* figure: descending three-note arpeggio symbolizing Christ on the Mount of Olives.
  a. Suite No. 4 in E♭ Major, Prelude.
  b. *St. Matthew Passion*, recitative ("The Savior falls down before his Father").
  c. Heinrich Ignaz Franz Biber, Mystery Sonata No. 6 ("Christ on the Mount of Olives").

Such three-note falling arpeggios, especially when following a rest, sometimes appear in German Baroque music to represent the Fall of sinful humankind and more specifically Christ on the Mount of Olives contemplating the impending Crucifixion (see Example 2.14).[47] If the Prelude's opening represents a contemplation of the Fall from innocence, this notion might be represented musically when the purity of the opening tonic triad (mm. 1–2) is disturbed with the entrance of the dissonant d♭' (mm. 3–4). Schachter writes:

> In the music of mm. 1–10, the jaggedly descending arpeggios, the D♭ falling to C... and the consequent lack of a D♮ rising to E♭ in the proper high register might then all stand for the fall of sinful humanity. The systematic introduction of rising accidentals that permeates the next phase could represent steps in the believer's path toward salvation. This spiritual journey involves a contemplation of the Cross, symbolized by the advent of C♯ [in m. 49], which transforms the initial falling chromatic sound into one that rises. After the G-minor cadence [in m. 62], the music introduces lowered accidentals, a process that culminates in the cadential Neapolitan chord and the [structural cadence in m. 82]. ... These tonal events might suggest mortality and physical death, but they are mitigated by the final rise to the high E♭, the saved soul's ascent to heaven.[48]

Schachter's interpretation is rooted in the enharmonic association of D♭ (mm. 3–4, representing humankind's Fall) and C♯ (m. 49, representing salvation through the Crucifixion).[49] It further relies on the double meaning of the German word "Kreuz," which in musical contexts means "sharp" but otherwise means "cross," an association that Bach exploits in some texted music with texts relating to the Crucifixion; see Bach's settings of "Kreuz" (and its derivatives) in *Christ lag in Todesbanden* (BWV4) and in the Passions.[50] Interpreting the fermata C♯ as Crucifixion accords with the painful harmonic intensity and the arduous, agonizing quality of the music that follows (mm. 49–61), as well as with the tremendous emphasis placed on D♮ in the cadenzas leading to the final cadence (mm. 88–90). The earlier emphasis on a falling D♭ is thus compensated for with the ebullient rise of D♮, as leading tone, to the final tonic chord, restoring the harmonic purity of the Prelude's opening.

Allemande

The ensuing five movements follow a basic design found in many major-mode dances across Bach's instrumental suites. Cast in a two-reprise form (also known as "binary form"), each dance begins with a first reprise (or "A" section) that introduces its main melodic idea and ends with a modulation to the dominant key. The second reprise (or "B" section) opens with a restatement of the main idea emphasizing the dominant harmony, followed by modulations to one or more minor keys (often the submediant), and closing with a return to the tonic. Each of these modulations is marked with a cadence, often using similar melodic material that marks these arrivals for special attention. This same formal design is found in suites in minor keys but with some adjustments to the key scheme of the modulations. Like milestones on a journey, the three principal cadences of a dance movement represent important arrivals. The nature of the music between these goals – whether the path is easy or fraught, the modulations gradual or abrupt, the cadences straightforward or delayed by complications – characterizes a movement's expressive trajectory.

The Allemande is a textbook example of this design. The main idea is characterized by the ascending leap from upbeat to downbeat, inaugurating an opening section emphasizing the tonic key (mm. 1–6). The remainder of the reprise is composed largely of sequences emphasizing the note A♮, the leading tone of the dominant key. A charming detail occurs in m. 13, when the movement nearly arrives prematurely at the dominant-key cadence – expressed with a melody of D–C–B♭ over beats 1–3 – but the phrase seems suddenly to change its mind, tumbling ahead into one final sequence before arriving at the true reprise-ending cadence in m. 16.

The second reprise opens with a dominant-key restatement of the main idea, a statement that reintroduces A♭ so as to effect a fleeting return to the tonic (mm. 17–18).[51] The ensuing material emphasizes the note B♮, pivoting toward the key of C minor for the intermediate cadence in m. 22. That cadence is strongly marked by the wide leaps between bass and melody, the use of open strings for the cadential bass line (G–C), and the four-note chord at the cadential arrival. All of these features suggest a sense of effort or intensity at this juncture. The movement makes weaker cadences (or resting points) in two other minor keys: G minor (m. 26) and F minor (m. 28), both marked with figures recalling the cadence of the first reprise (m. 16).

The remainder of the Allemande is concerned with a return to the tonic. One noteworthy detail is the D♭ in m. 32; the introduction of a flattened seventh (often transforming the tonic triad into a dominant seventh) is common toward the end of second reprises, as part of a flatward shift on the circle of fifths that emphasizes the subdominant and signals that the movement is approaching its close.⁵² Throughout this suite, the many dances that feature D♭s toward the end of their second reprises may also be related motivically to the special role of D♭ in the openings of several movements (see Example 2.10).

Courante

The Courante's unusual variety of rhythms – stately eighth notes punctuated by scampering sixteenth-note "lead-in" gestures and flowing triplets – suggests a playful character. The first reprise is subdivided into an opening section that remains in the orbit of the tonic key (mm. 1–8) followed by a second part that achieves the modulation to the dominant (mm. 9–26). The music leading to the first cadence in B♭ invites a crescendo as successively higher statements of the same figure increase the intensity: a third interval (m. 18), then a sixth (m. 19), then strengthened as a three-note chord (m. 20), and finally boosted with a G–F appoggiatura (m. 21). After this strenuous path to the main cadence (achieved in m. 23), at hard-won cadence, the return of the scampering sixteenths ushers in a lighter codetta that confirms the cadence an octave lower (m. 27).

The second reprise swerves immediately toward the submediant, with a cadence (as in the Allemande) marked by large, "effortful" leaps (mm. 40–42). As in the Allemande, the Courante's return to the tonic places some passing emphasis on D♭ toward the end of the second reprise (mm. 50–51). The music leading to the tonic-key cadences that close the movement (mm. 56–64) is exactly parallel to the corresponding music from the end of the first reprise (mm. 18–26). This element of "end rhyme" – with corresponding material closing both reprises – is a common feature of Bach's dance movements.⁵³

Sarabande

The Sarabande opens with an emphasis on D♭ that recalls the Prelude (see Example 2.10). That D♭ is the first statement of this Sarabande's characteristic figure: a suspension prepared on a third beat that is either tied over or restruck on the following downbeat,

Analysis of Suite No. 4

resolving on the second beat. The many such suspensions, usually combined with the rhythm ♩♫♫♩, are a fingerprint of this elegant movement.

The moderate tempo of Bach's cello sarabandes tends to allow for more chordal writing than is found in faster dances. Here, the density of three-note chords (mm. 15–18) and the hemiola figure (mm. 18–19) intensify the modulation to the submediant (confirmed cadentially in m. 20). The ensuing reduction in chordal density with the return to the tonic suggests some relaxation (mm. 21–24). Starting in m. 25, the Sarabande seems poised to follow the end-rhyme strategy: The same music that in the first reprise led to a cadence in B♭ (mm. 9–12) now returns in E♭, implying that a final cadence should be achieved four bars later. But m. 28 instead expresses a deceptive resolution, motivating a second, successful attempt to achieve a cadence in E♭ in mm. 29–32.

Bourrées I and II

After the reflective Sarabande, the Bourrée I infuses the suite with newfound energy immediately from its sixteenth-note upbeat gesture. It follows the same formal design with three principal cadences: in the dominant at the end of the first reprise (m. 12), in the submediant in the middle of the second reprise (m. 22), and finally in tonic at the end (m. 48). The four bars leading to each of these cadences use parallel material, expressing the idea of "end rhyme." The movement includes various repetitions (such as in mm. 5–8) that seem to call for dynamic echo effects; such dynamic effects are indicated in some manuscript sources and probably should be observed throughout. The second reprise also features the perorational emphasis in D♭ found in several other movements (mm. 29–30).

The Bourrée II is a rare instance in the Cello Suites where the cello plays a duet with itself, with a fully fleshed-out melody and bass line (compare to the Andante from the Solo Violin Sonata No. 2 in A Minor, BWV1003). In the bars without double stops, the registers tend to distinguish melody from bass, an effect that can be enhanced in performance with distinct articulation and tone color for each part.

Dance Types, Preludes, and Analytical Perspectives

Gigue

The sprightly Gigue is composed nearly as a *moto perpetuo* finale. Despite the relatively homogeneous surface rhythms, various features invite the performer to articulate certain junctures. For instance, the repetition in mm. 3–6 suggests an echo effect, and the discontinuation of that effect serves to mark mm. 7–10 as the cadential phrase that achieves an arrival in B♭.

The second reprise opens parallel to the first, with a dominant-key restatement of the main idea (mm. 11–12) followed by a return of the echo-repetition idea (mm. 13–14). The following four bars (mm. 15–18) achieve a modulation to and cadence in the submediant. This cadence, which turns out to be the first of two intermediate cadences in minor keys, is marked by a ritornello-style return of the main idea in C minor (starting in m. 19), except that the sudden introduction of F♯ (starting in m. 20) effects an abrupt "plot twist" that swerves toward G minor, arriving at the second intermediate cadence in m. 26.

As if correcting for the consecutive minor-key cadences, the ensuing recapitulation (m. 27) constitutes a double return of the main idea and the tonic key. As is common in recapitulations, it places some emphasis on the flattened seventh (D♭, mm. 31–32). The reprise's final four bars (mm. 39–42) are parallel to those of the first reprise (mm. 7–10), closing the Gigue (and the suite) with brilliance and end rhyme.

Notes

1. Wolff, *Bach: The Learned Musician*, 333–34. For a wider study of sources on Bach and Baroque dance, see also Little and Jenne, *Dance and the Music of J. S. Bach*.
2. Ernst Ludwig Gerber, *Historisch-Biographisches Lexikon der Tonkünstler*, 2 vols. (Leipzig, 1790–92), 1:492.
3. Johann Philipp Kirnberger, *Recueil d'airs de danse caractéristiques* (Berlin, c. 1777), 1–2.
4. David, Mendel, and Wolff, *New Bach Reader*, 448. For a penetrating reflection on this passage, see John Butt, "Bach and the Dance of Humankind," in *Musicology and Dance: Historical and Critical Perspectives*, ed. Davinia Caddy and Maribeth Clark (Cambridge: Cambridge University Press, 2020), 19–48.

Analysis of Suite No. 4

5. Walther, *Musicalisches Lexikon*, 28.
6. Johann Mattheson, *Johann Mattheson's "Der vollkommene Capellmeister": A Revised Translation with Critical Commentary*, trans. Ernest Charles Harriss (Ann Arbor: UMI Research Press, 1981), 464.
7. Mattheson, *Das neu-eröffnete Orchestre*, 185–86. Walther, *Musicalisches Lexikon*, 27.
8. See Marin Mersenne, *Harmonie universelle*, 2 vols. (Paris, 1636–37), 1:164–65.
9. See Gottfried Tauber, *Rechtschaffener Tanzmeister, oder gründliche Erklärung der frantzösischen Tantz-Künst*, 3 vols. (Leipzig, 1717), 2:570.
10. Mattheson, *Das neu-eröffnete Orchestre*, 186.
11. Mattheson, *Der vollkommene Capellmeister*, 462.
12. Kirnberger, *Recueil d'airs de danse caractéristiques*, 2.
13. Walther, *Musicalisches Lexikon*, 542.
14. Mattheson, *Der vollkommene Capellmeister*, 461.
15. On the relationship between meter signatures and tempo, see Roger Matthew Grant, *Beating Time & Measuring Music in the Early Modern Era* (Oxford: Oxford University Press, 2014), 125–46. For a delightfully extreme case, see the Lilliputian Chaconne (in $\frac{3}{32}$) and the Brobdingnagian Gigue (in $\frac{24}{1}$) in Telemann's *Gulliver's Travels Suite* (TWV40:108).
16. On the *saltus duriusculus* (harsh or dissonant leap), see Dietrich Bartel, *Musica Poetica: Musical-Rhetorical Figures in German Baroque Music* (Lincoln, NE: University of Nebraska Press, 1997), 381–82.
17. Mattheson, *Das neu-eröffnete Orchestre*, 193.
18. Joseph Riepel's 1752 treatise on composing minuets is excerpted in Leo Treitler, ed., *Strunk's Source Readings in Music History*, rev. ed. (New York: W. W. Norton, 1998), 749–61.
19. Walther, *Musicalisches Lexikon*, 398.
20. Mattheson, *Der vollkommene Capellmeister*, 451.
21. Eric McKee, *Decorum of the Minuet, Delirium of the Waltz: A Study of Dance-Music Relations in $\frac{3}{4}$ Time* (Bloomington: Indiana University Press, 2013), 15–45.
22. Mattheson, *Der vollkommene Capellmeister*, 454.
23. Mattheson, *Der vollkommene Capellmeister*, 454.
24. Walther, *Musicalisches Lexikon*, 110.
25. See Meredith Ellis Little, "Gavotte," in *Grove Music Online*, rev. Matthew Werley, ed. Deane Root (published January 20, 2001; rev. September 3, 2014).
26. Mattheson, *Der vollkommene Capellmeister*, 453.
27. See Grant, *Beating Time*, 115–17.

28. Carl Schachter, *The Art of Tonal Analysis: Twelve Lessons in Schenkerian Analysis*, ed. Joseph N. Straus (Oxford: Oxford University Press, 2015), 104–6.
29. Mattheson, *Der vollkommene Capellmeister*, 457.
30. Thomas Mace, *Musick's Monument; or, A Remembrancer of the Best Practical Musick* (London, 1676), 120. "Voluntary play" refers to improvisation (p. 115). "Toy" denotes a seventeenth-century genre similar to the gigue/jig: "*Toys*, or *Jiggs*, are *Light-Squibbish Things*, only fit for *Fantastical*, and *Easie-Light-Headed People*; and are of any sort of *Time*" (p. 129).
31. Martin Heinrich Fuhrmann, *Musicalischer-Trichter* (Frankfurt, 1706), 87.
32. Walther, *Musicalisches Lexikon*, 128.
33. Friedrich Erhard Niedt's *Handleitung zur Variation* (Hamburg, 1706) is the second volume of a three-part treatise titled *Musicalische Handleitung* (1700–1717). On his method of composing suites, see Niedt, *The Musical Guide: Parts I (1700/10), II (1721), and III (1717)*, trans. Pamela L. Poulin and Irmgard C. Taylor (Oxford: Clarendon Press, 1989), 155–78. On Niedt's possible influence on the Bach circle, see David Schulenberg, "Composition as Variation: Inquiries into the Compositional Procedures of the Bach Circle of Composers," *Current Musicology* 33 (1982): 57–87; and Schulenberg, "Composition and Improvisation in the School of J. S. Bach," in *Bach Perspectives 1*, ed. Russell Stinson (Lincoln, NE: University of Nebraska Press, 1995), 7–13.
34. Niedt, *The Musical Guide*, 178.
35. On variation suites, see David Fuller, "Suite," in *Grove Music Online*, ed. Dean Root (published January 20, 2001), section 6 ("the classical suite after the addition of the gigue"). On Bach's early keyboard variation suites, see Schulenberg, *The Keyboard Music of J. S. Bach*, 49–56.
36. Pamela L. Poulin, trans., *J. S. Bach's Precepts and Principles for Playing the Thorough-Bass or Accompanying in Four Parts: Leipzig, 1738* (Oxford: Clarendon Press, 1994), xiii–xix.
37. On a similar unifying progression in Bach's Solo Violin Partita No. 2, see Joel Lester, "J. S. Bach Teaches Us How to Compose: Four Pattern Preludes from the *Well-Tempered Clavier*," *College Music Symposium* 38 (1998): 40–41.
38. On a similar characteristic sonority in Bach's Solo Violin Sonata No. 1, see Joel Lester, *Bach's Works for Solo Violin: Style, Structure, Performance* (Oxford: Oxford University Press, 1999), 3–4.
39. This analysis of the scalar motive in Suite No. 3 is adapted from Irit Youngerman, "J. S. Bach's Suite in C Major for Violoncello Solo:

An Analysis through Application of a Historical Approach" (MM thesis, University of Cincinnati, 2002), 14–20.
40. For a more cautious view about cyclic elements in Bach's suites, see Schulenberg, *The Keyboard Music of J. S. Bach*, 42.
41. C. P. E. Bach, *Essay on the True Art of Playing Keyboard Instruments*, trans. and ed. William J. Mitchell (New York: W. W. Norton, 1949), 431.
42. C. P. E. Bach, *Essay*, 431–34.
43. For an illustration of how Bach's compositional methods might be gleaned from analysis of selected keyboard preludes, see Lester, "J. S. Bach Teaches Us How to Compose."
44. On "durational reduction" as an analytical method, see Carl Schachter, "Rhythm and Linear Analysis: Durational Reduction," in *Unfoldings: Essays in Schenkerian Theory and Analysis*, ed. Joseph N. Straus (Oxford: Oxford University Press, 1999), 54–78.
45. Carl Schachter, "The Prelude from Bach's Suite No. 4 for Violoncello Solo: The Submerged Urlinie," *Current Musicology* 56 (1994): 54–71.
46. For a speculative reading of Christian symbolism across the Cello Suites, see also Steven Isserlis, *The Bach Cello Suites: A Companion* (London: Faber & Faber, 2021), 111–44.
47. Colin Lawson and Robin Stowell, *The Historical Performance of Music: An Introduction* (Cambridge: Cambridge University Press, 1999), 31.
48. Schachter, "The Prelude from Bach's Suite No. 4," 70–71.
49. On enharmonic associations in music analysis, see Patrick McCreless, "The Pitch-Class Motive in Tonal Analysis: Some Historical and Critical Observations," *Res Musica* 3 (2011): 52–68.
50. On the word-painting in the Passions, see John Butt, *Bach's Dialogue with Modernity: Perspectives on the Passions* (Cambridge: Cambridge University Press, 2010), 167–70.
51. On the "V–I schema" that commonly opens Bach's second reprises, see Christopher Brody, "Second-Reprise Opening Schemas in Bach's Binary Movements," *Music Theory Spectrum* 43, no. 2 (Fall 2021): 257–79.
52. Yoel Greenberg, *How Sonata Forms: A Bottom-Up Approach to Musical Form* (Oxford: Oxford University Press, 2022), 110–11.
53. Greenberg, *How Sonata Forms*, 79–82.

3

THE FOUR MANUSCRIPT COPIES

Performers of Bach's Violin Solos can choose to consult the calligraphic autograph manuscript; an *Urtext* edition, which faithfully transmits the same essential text (notes, rhythms, slurs, and embellishments); or a performance edition reflecting a prominent musician's interpretive approach (bowing, fingers, dynamics, metronome markings, etc.). But a vexing problem for performers of the Cello Suites is the lack of an authoritative text, meaning that various cellists may use wildly divergent slur articulations and bowings, embellishments, and in some passages even different notes. This chapter surveys why this is the case and offers some perspectives to guide musicians in interpreting published editions or creating their own performance editions. For a more complete account of textual and editorial questions about the Cello Suites – which continue to evolve with new insights each decade – readers should consult the critical reports of the latest scholarly editions. This chapter is heavily indebted to pathbreaking research by Andrew Talle, whose edition of the Cello Suites presents a new view of the relationships among the manuscript sources, thus offering a major advance on all prior editions.

Unless the autograph manuscript were someday to miraculously resurface, the text of the Cello Suites will never be as clear as that of the Violin Solos. Even if the lost autograph were found, it is doubtful that Bach ever produced a fair copy of the Cello Suites equivalent in its precision and finality to that of the Violin Solos. In sum, the textual problems of the Cello Suites resist simple solutions, but understanding these issues can empower musicians to make interpretive decisions with greater confidence.

Over 100 published editions of the Cello Suites have appeared over the past two centuries, according to a recent

The Four Manuscript Copies

Example 3.1 Suite No. 1 in G Major, Prelude: The four manuscript copies. Reproduced by permission of the Berlin State Library and the Austrian National Library.
    a. Anna Magdalena Bach (Source A).
    b. Johann Peter Kellner (Source B).
    c. Johann Nikolaus Schober (Source C, first half).
    d. Anonymous Hamburg copyist (Source D).

estimate.[1] All of them trace back to the four surviving eighteenth-century manuscript sources, which are widely available both in facsimile editions and online, and which musicians routinely consult to guide their performance choices.[2] The first two (designated Sources A and B) date from Bach's lifetime, and the latter two (Sources C and D) were made several decades later (see Example 3.1).

The Four Manuscript Copies

Source A: Anna Magdalena Bach
(Berlin State Library, P269)

The composer's second wife, Anna Magdalena Bach, made this copy c. 1727–31. It was originally the second half of a two-part manuscript comprising both the Violin Solos and the Cello Suites, which she copied at Schwanberger's request. The sense of a two-part collection is captured on the title page written in Schwanberger's hand:

Pars 1 | Violino Solo | Senza Basso | composée | par | Sr. Jean Seb: Bach.
Pars 2 | Violoncello Solo. | Senza Basso | composée | par | Sr. J. S. Bach. | Maitre de la Chapelle | et | Directeur de la Musique | a | Leipsic. | ecrite par Madame | Bachen son Epouse.

Although this title page originally referred to both the violin and cello works, at some point the manuscript's two parts were separated, and Schwanberger added a separate title page specifically for the Cello Suites:

6 | Suites a | Violoncello Solo | senza | Basso | composées | par | Sr J. S. Bach. | Maitre de Chapelle.

Since Anna Magdalena Bach's copy of the Violin Solos is clearly modeled after her husband's calligraphic autograph manuscript, it has long been assumed that she likewise copied the Cello Suites from an autograph. However, more recent scholarship has concluded that it was most likely based on an intermediate copy by another scribe in Bach's circle.[3] Talle outlines the following plausible scenario:

[The autograph] was unusually sloppy in character, more of a working draft than a fair copy. Perhaps it was also damaged or fragmentary (e.g., separate suites or even movements may have been bundled individually) in a way that made it impractical for the composer to loan ... [the autograph] to musicians eager to know this music. The composer probably requested that a student or colleague make a clean copy of ... [the autograph] and encouraged his wife and others to use this manuscript as a model for subsequent copies.[4]

Talle's hypothesis would also explain the autograph's disappearance, since the composer might have considered his messy, damaged, or fragmentary composing draft to have been effectively replaced by the fair copy he apparently requested.

Source B: Johann Peter Kellner

What sort of a copyist was Anna Magdalena Bach? Reportedly an "outstanding soprano" who commanded an unusually high salary as a member of the Cöthen court Capelle,[5] she was without question a highly accomplished professional musician in her own right.[6] She was, however, neither a professional copyist nor a string player, and the many errors and inconsistencies found in her manuscripts may reflect a combination of factors, including the quality of her exemplars, her speed of work, and more generally the challenges of balancing copying work with other musical and domestic responsibilities. Yo Tomita observes that, "as a mother who became pregnant almost every year in the first ten years of her marriage, as well as looking after children, one can imagine how difficult it must have been for her to maintain her focus for long periods of time" while undertaking scribal work.[7] Indeed, a comparison of her manuscript of the Violin Solos with her husband's autograph reveals her inconsistencies and lack of clarity, notably in the imprecise or inaccurate notation of slurs, markings that string players rely on to indicate bowings and articulations (see Example 3.2).

Talle's meticulous study of Anna Magdalena Bach's copy of the Cello Suites "reveals beyond a reasonable doubt that she could not have been hearing the notes and rhythms in her head" but instead copied the manuscript mechanically. Talle cites a number of eccentricities in her copy – such as measures missing beats or containing extra notes, errors in the copying of appoggiaturas and grace notes, and an incorrect movement title for the Allemande from Suite No. 5 – that are consistent with rote copying rather than audiation.[8] It is unknown whether these errors were introduced by Anna Magdalena Bach or whether some of them may have been present in her source; nevertheless, a professional copyist working slowly and without distractions would presumably have noticed and corrected some of the more egregious mistakes.

Source B: Johann Peter Kellner
(Berlin State Library, P804)

The Thuringian organist Johann Peter Kellner (1705–72) was a prolific copyist of Bach's instrumental music. Kellner apparently

The Four Manuscript Copies

Example 3.2 Violin Solos, comparing slurs in manuscripts by J. S. Bach and Anna Magdalena Bach. Reproduced by permission of the Berlin State Library.
    a. Sonata No. 1 in G Minor, Adagio (m. 6).
      1 J. S. Bach (autograph).
  2 Anna Magdalena (missing slur in beat 1, misplaced/missing slur in beat 4).

had some contact with Bach after c. 1727, possibly as his student, although the precise nature of their relationship is unknown. The two musicians had several common acquaintants, who must have provided Kellner access to manuscript copies of Bach's music, and some of his later manuscripts may even have been made from autographs.[9] Despite the significance of Kellner's collecting and copying in the early transmission of Bach's instrumental music, his manuscripts are nevertheless not known for their accuracy. Many include not only common errors (wrong notes and rhythms, missing notes or even measures) but also more substantial eccentricities (omission or abridgment of individual movements, arising either from Kellner's intentional alteration of his sources or else through scribal corruption).[10]

    Kellner's music library is preserved in a nearly 400-page miscellany volume comprising dozens of individual manuscripts,

Source B: Johann Peter Kellner

Example 3.2 (Cont.)
b. Partita No. 1 in B Minor, Tempo di Borea (m. 58).
   1 J. S. Bach (autograph).
   2 Anna Magdalena Bach (inaccurate slurs).

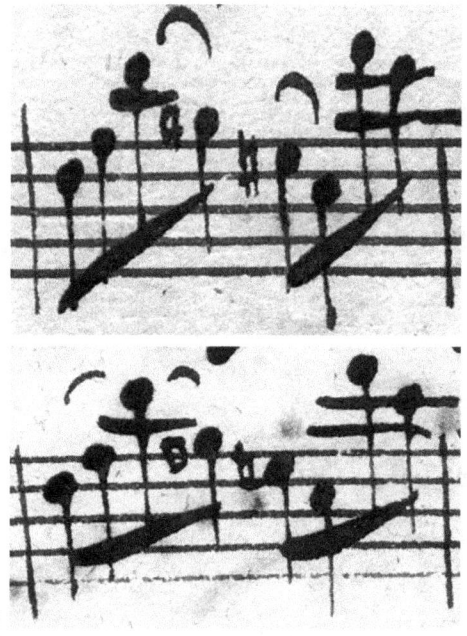

primarily keyboard and organ music but also his copies of Bach's Violin Solos and Cello Suites.[11] Since Kellner's copies of the Violin Solos and Cello Suites use similar handwriting and paper types, it is likely that both were copied from the same source and around the same time – in 1726, according to Kellner's inscription at the end of the Violin Solos manuscript. If the assumption that Kellner's copy of the Cello Suites likewise dates from 1726 is correct, then it would be the earliest surviving source.

Since Bach is unlikely to have loaned his autograph to a twenty-one-year-old who was unknown to him at the time, Kellner's exemplar must have been some other (now lost) manuscript copy. Talle suggests, plausibly, that Kellner may have obtained such a manuscript from the composer's nephew, student, and former copyist Johann Bernhard Bach der Jüngere ("the

Example 3.2 (Cont.)
c. Sonata No. 2 in A Minor, Andante (m. 9).
1 J. S. Bach (autograph).
2 Anna Magdalena Bach (first two beats only: vague slur on beat 2, resulting from "wide" quarter rest in the lower voice).

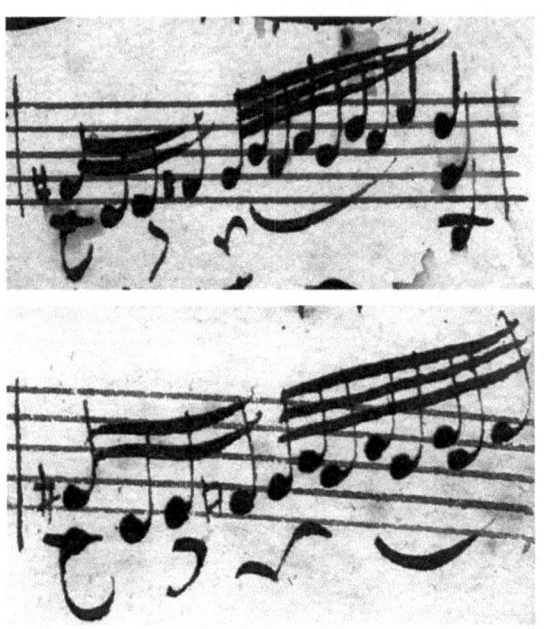

Younger") (1700–1743), who resided near Kellner around the time the latter prepared the violin and cello manuscripts.[12]

A virtuoso organist, Kellner might have had some proficiency on violin but did not play the cello.[13] His manuscript copies of the Violin Solos and Cello Suites seem to have been made primarily as reference copies and/or for performance on keyboard rather than violin or cello.[14] Whereas all other Cello Suites sources indicate the title as "suites" and the instrument as "violoncello," Kellner's manuscript bears the following peculiar, mixed-language title:

Sechs Suonaten | Pour le [*sic*] Viola de Basso | par Jean Sebastian | Bach: | pos. | Johann Peter Kellner

Source B: Johann Peter Kellner

Example 3.2 (Cont.)
d. Partita No. 2 in D minor, Allemande (m. 2).
1 J. S. Bach (autograph).
2 Anna Magdalena Bach (slurs misplaced in beats 1–2, slur missing at end of bar).

Despite the term "Suonaten" on the title page, throughout the manuscript each piece is nevertheless identified as a "Suitte." Kellner may have considered "sonatas" to be a more modern designation than "suites"; as noted in Chapter 1, C. P. E. Bach likewise referred to the Cello Suites as sonatas in his coauthored obituary, even though he possessed a manuscript copy in which they were identified as suites. "Viola de basso" or "viola bassa" were essentially synonyms for "violoncello," but it is curious that Kellner opted for a term not found in any other surviving manuscript. The indication "pos. Johann Peter Kellner" identifies Kellner as the owner of the manuscript, confirming that he copied it for his own use.

Talle observes that "Kellner deliberately left out much information specifically pertaining to string playing" found in all other sources, notably the indications for *scordatura* in Suite No. 5 and for a five-string instrument for Suite No. 6.[15] The case of Suite No. 5 is especially telling. All other sources notate that suite in *Griffbrett* notation, showing the fingerings to be used on a cello tuned *scordatura* – that is, notes on the cello's top string are notated one tone higher than they will sound in performance. But Kellner attempted (with mixed success) to notate his copy at sounding pitch, a choice that made his manuscript well suited for keyboard playing but virtually useless for a cello performance of Suite No. 5. Consider, for example, m. 2 of the Prelude: Kellner notates the chord C–B–f–a♭, which is unplayable on a cello in standard (non-*scordatura*) tuning since the top two notes would both be on the same string. The other sources provide indications for the cellist to tune their instrument *scordatura*, thus enabling that four-note chord to be playable with the a♭ on the top string.

Curiously, Kellner's copy abridges Suite No. 5, omitting the Sarabande completely and cutting off the Gigue after just eight measures.[16] Such truncation might reflect his considerable difficulty translating his *Griffbrett* model into a sounding-pitch copy. Another possibility is that he might have considered the Sarabande and Gigue to be less interesting than the other movements of Suite No. 5 for his purposes as a keyboard player since they are the only two that do not employ chordal writing.

Source C: Johann Nikolaus Schober and an Anonymous Colleague (Berlin State Library, P289)

Despite being written more neatly and clearly and containing more detailed performance indications than the earlier two manuscripts, Sources C and D have attracted less attention from performers and scholarly editors alike, owing to their greater distance from the composer both temporally and geographically as well as to the long-standing anonymity of their scribes. However, the value of Source C has been reconsidered over the past few decades since Johann Nikolaus Schober (c. 1721–1807) was recently identified as the scribe of the manuscript's first half (up through the middle of Suite No. 3, Bourrée I), with an unknown colleague completing the remainder.[17] A horn player and copyist at the Prussian court in Berlin starting in 1757, Schober must have had close contact with C. P. E. Bach, who was harpsichordist at the Prussian court until 1768.

C. P. E. Bach is known to have owned a manuscript copy of the Cello Suites; his estate catalog includes an entry for "6 handwritten suites for violoncello without bass, bound."[18] We can assume that sometime around 1760 he commissioned Schober to make a copy of his treasured manuscript and subsequently engaged another copyist to complete the job that Schober (for whatever reason) had left unfinished. Whereas Ulrich Leisinger speculates that the copy in C. P. E. Bach's possession may have been a second autograph, Talle argues convincingly that it contained errors that could not have been made by the composer, concluding therefore that it was a manuscript prepared within the composer's circle, possibly with autograph annotations.[19] C. P. E. Bach nevertheless considered it to be sufficiently authoritative to be used as a model for a subsequent copy. Source C is sometimes nicknamed the "Westphal" copy since it belonged at one point to the Hamburg organist and music dealer Johann Christian Westphal, who likely received or purchased it from C. P. E. Bach.

Source D: Anonymous Hamburg Copyist
(Austrian National Library, Mus. Hs. 5007)

This copy was prepared by a single copyist working in Hamburg around 1790–1800. Although the scribe's identity is unknown, his handwriting matches that found in a set of string parts for a concerto by C. P. E. Bach, commissioned in 1795 by his daughter Anna Carolina Philippina (1747–1804). A letter dating from the same year records her high regard for the copyist in question.[20] Leisinger and Talle propose the following scenario: C. P. E. Bach must have brought his copy of the Cello Suites with him when he quit Berlin for Hamburg in 1768, since he still possessed it upon his death in 1788. The subsequent publication of his estate catalog in 1790, which listed his copy of the manuscript, must have attracted the attention of the Viennese music publisher and Bach enthusiast Johann Traeg (1747–1805), who would have contacted A. C. P. Bach in Hamburg to request a copy. This, in turn, would have prompted her to commission her esteemed Hamburg scribe as copyist.[21]

Making Sense of the Sources

If – as Talle demonstrates – none of the four surviving manuscript sources was copied directly from an autograph,[22] how are we to grapple with their many divergent readings, especially of slurs, articulations, embellishments, and sometimes notes and rhythms? Most cellists and editors have opted to focus on a single source that they regard as the most authoritative, consulting others only as needed to clarify matters of doubt. Anna Magdalena Bach's copy (Source A) has traditionally attracted special interest, based on the premise that her intimate proximity to the composer confers a certain authenticity; indeed, many cellists have regarded it as essentially a surrogate for the lost autograph. Moreover, whereas Kellner's and Schober's names are familiar only to a narrow circle of Bach researchers, Anna Magdalena Bach is widely known by musicians since pieces from the *Little Notebook for Anna Magdalena Bach* have long been used for elementary piano instruction.

Perhaps the most devoted evangelist for her copy was the influential Baroque cellist Anner Bylsma (1934–2019). His highly personal study of the manuscript revels in its idiosyncrasies, arguing that they should be observed precisely in performance, even when they result in unusual "backwards" bowings (e.g., chords on up bows, inconsistent bowings in sequential passages, etc.): "My guess is that the notes in the manuscript are by Mrs. Bach, and that the slurs may be in the hand of her husband. All of the slurs are clearly marked."[23] Bylsma's claim about the clarity of the slur markings in Source A is squarely at odds with widespread opinion – among musicians and editors alike – that it is "somewhat carelessly written, particularly as regards slurs."[24] In a philosophical approach similar to Bylsma's, cellist Matt Haimovitz (b. 1970) titled his second recording of the Cello Suites *J. S. Bach: The Cello Suites According to Anna Magdalena*, advertising his intention to adhere closely to the details of this specific manuscript.[25]

Making Sense of the Sources

Example 3.3 Suite No. 2 in D Minor, Menuet I, variant readings in mm. 6–7.

Such fastidious fidelity to the finest details of a specific manuscript copy source can make for compellingly original and innovative performances, but it is unlikely that any eighteenth-century cellist would have adopted this viewpoint rooted in post-Romantic and modernist notions of faithfulness to a musical text (*Werktreue*).[26] Treatises by Quantz and Mozart, for example, reveal that mid eighteenth-century musicians sometimes exercised discretion to add slurs as needed to adopt a uniform bowing in sequences or other passages with repeated figures.[27] Other eighteenth-century treatises likewise discuss how musicians may add slurs, at their discretion, to support the character of the music. Moreover, given the many discrepancies between Anna Magdalena Bach's copy of the Violin Solos and the surviving autograph (as shown in Example 3.2), it is demonstrably clear that her manuscript of the Cello Suites could not mirror her husband's lost autograph so closely as to oblige strict adherence to its every detail and quirk.

Departing from the long-standing focus on Anna Magdalena Bach's manuscript as a primary source, some researchers and musicians have recently reappraised the other sources' merits. The cellist and musicologist Zoltán Szabó argues for the priority of Kellner's copy, based on his speculation that its variant readings stem not from Kellner's carelessness or willful alteration but rather from his exemplar being "a more mature version of the suites than any to which other copyists had access."[28] A favorite example of Szabó's – where Kellner's reading diverges markedly from the other sources – is shown in Example 3.3. Another advocate of Kellner's manuscript is cellist Martin Rummel (b. 1974), who released an album advertised as the first to follow that source specifically.[29] Leisinger's edition, on the other hand, is based entirely on the long-neglected Sources C and D. Both manuscripts were prepared by professional copyists working from the copy once owned by C. P. E. Bach, which Leisinger assumes was a second autograph.[30]

Although both Szabó and Leisinger deserve credit for motivating new debates by questioning long-standing conventional wisdom, several of their arguments have been corrected by Talle. Szabó's theory that Kellner had access to a second, more mature autograph is undercut by the many errors common to all four sources, suggesting that they all stem ultimately from a single ancestor autograph.[31] These common errors found in all four surviving sources likewise cast doubt on Leisinger's theory that the exemplar for Sources C and D – the copy belonging to C. P. E. Bach – was a second autograph, since it is implausible that the composer could have repeated so many mistakes in two separate autographs.[32]

Talle's edition adopts the most reasonable editorial philosophy – if not the simplest – by considering carefully what useful information can be gleaned from each of the four sources, given what is known about their copyists and the circumstances of their creation. With respect to the slur markings, which are notoriously inconsistent and difficult to interpret in all sources, Talle evaluates the reliability of Anna Magdalena Bach (Source A), Kellner (Source B), and Schober (first half of Source C) based on their respective copies of the Violin Solos.[33] He reports that Anna Magdalena Bach's copy includes 85 percent of the slurs in her husband's autograph, Kellner only 58 percent, and Schober an impressive 97 percent. Talle concludes that the bowings in Schober's portion of Source C can be assumed to be more reliable than those in Sources A and B. He adds: "None of these scribes was in the habit of inventing new slurs. When a slur appears in Sources A, B, or Schober's portion of Source C, we can assume that it appeared in their model, if not always in the same way."[34]

A second issue is the variety of performance indications – ornaments (trills, mordents, appoggiaturas), articulations (dots, strokes), dynamics, and tempo markings – that are found in

Sources B, C, and D but are absent in Source A. Talle argues convincingly that these embellishments or clarifications are best explained by Bach's documented habit of initially composing a piece in a basic, lightly ornamented version and subsequently adding additional embellishments and articulation markings in later copies. Bach entered various embellishments in his autographs or his students' copies of various keyboard music, such as the Inventions, Sinfonias, and French Suites. Another illustrative example is the French Ouverture, which is best known in its heavily ornamented final version (BWV831, published 1735) but which also survives in an earlier, manuscript version with fewer ornaments and articulation markings (BWV831a).[35]

For the Cello Suites, evidence for a trajectory from a simpler original (preserved by Anna Magdalena Bach) toward a more richly embellished later version is found in the composer's own transcription of Suite No. 5 for lute in G minor (BWV995), prepared between 1727 and 1732.[36] Sources B, C, and D transmit a middle stage in Bach's process of adding ornaments and clarifications, with the lute version representing the most elaborate stage. Talle argues compellingly that many of these additions likely originated with the composer, who might have added markings "during lessons or other musical interactions ... [that] responded to the needs of particular musicians ... [and that arose] organically within the context of music-making."[37]

The high degree of consistency among many markings added in Sources B, C, and D suggests that these additions and clarifications originate with the composer, as he is the only person who could have influenced both Kellner's exemplar (used for Source B) and the copy belonging to C. P. E. Bach (used for Sources C and D).[38] For example, whereas Anna Magdalena Bach's copy lacks any dynamic or tempo markings, the other three surviving sources all share some common dynamics (in the "echo" passages in the Bourrée I of Suite No. 4) and a common tempo marking (in the Allemande of Suite No. 6, marked "Adagio" in Source B and "Molto Adagio" in Sources C and D). In the autograph of his lute transcription of Suite No. 5, Bach marked the Prelude's fugue "très viste," meaning "very fast"; this tempo is not found in any of the cello sources. Kellner's copy of the Cello Suites (Source B) indicates "presto" for the Prelude of Suite No. 3; as this marking is found in no other surviving source, it is unclear whether it was present in Kellner's exemplar or whether he added it at his own initiative.

Talle documents a significant number of ornaments and articulation markings that are absent in Anna Magdalena Bach's copy but that are common to Sources B, C, and D.[39] Since it is implausible that these respective copyists could have independently added the same nuances and clarifications (dynamics, tempo designations, embellishments, and articulations), the only reasonable conclusion is that the composer must have influenced the exemplars for Source B and for Sources C and D, meaning that these markings should therefore be considered to be authentic.

In sum, Talle's edition represents the best possible reconstruction of the basic text of the lost autograph (in terms of notes, rhythms, and slurs), with the addition of other nuances and clarifications (dynamics, tempo designations, ornaments, dots, and strokes) that were added in many cases at the composer's initiative in later manuscript copies that served as models for Sources B, C, and D, or in the autograph lute transcription. Unlike an edition based on a single primary source, the editorial process for an edition such as Talle's necessarily involves considerable educated guesswork. If a slur or ornament appears in a given passage, should it be applied when parallel material appears elsewhere in the same movement? Should slurs that appear within sequences be applied consistently to each statement of a repeated figure? If an embellishment appears in some but not all of Sources B, C, and D, is it more likely that some copyists added it or that others neglected to include it?

Some cellists will inevitably feel disappointed by this aspect of guesswork, compared to the much more straightforward textual status of the Violin Solos. While the desire for a single "authentic" text is understandable, cellists might nevertheless be reassured by considering what can be learned from the differences among the surviving manuscript sources. Talle writes:

While it is unfortunate that Bach's autograph manuscript of the Cello Suites is lost, the surviving materials are in some respects more instructive. In the absence of a definitive text, performers and scholars who deal with this music are forced to grapple with the reality that eighteenth-century performance practice was extremely flexible. Musicians of the era added or subtracted ornaments and even entire passages at will. They felt little obligation to perform the movements of a given work completely or in sequence. As documented in the sources, the composer himself seems to have adjusted this music in reaction to specific performances by students or colleagues. . . . [My edition] is not a perfect reconstruction of the lost autograph; no editor can reasonably expect to attain such a goal. I have sought rather to offer users a reliable rendition of the fundamental text of the six Cello Suites and a sense for the possibilities the composer himself encouraged his musicians to explore.[40]

This point about musicians customizing the nuances of the Cello Suites to suit their individual playing styles should be understood in the context of the varied approaches to cello performance during Bach's lifetime – when many players retained the older "underhand" bow hold while others adopted the newer "overhand" hold, and some may have played smaller instruments "da spalla" while others used larger instruments held between the knees. Ultimately, modern-day performers of the Cello Suites might do well to abandon the (ultimately fruitless) search for a single text or ideal performance approach and instead embrace the freedom and variety of possibilities that Bach's students and contemporaries enjoyed.

Notes

1. Zoltán Szabó, "Precarious Presumptions and the 'Minority Report': Revisiting the Primary Sources of the Bach Cello Suites," *BACH* 45, no. 2 (2014): 1–33.
2. Facsimiles of the manuscript sources are included in Schwemer and Woodfull-Harris, *6 Suites a Violoncello Solo senza Basso*; and (in a synoptic format) in Talle, *Six Suites for Violoncello Solo*. Scans are also available online through the International Music Score Library Project (http://imslp.org) and through Bach Digital (www.bach-digital.de).
3. James Grier, *The Critical Editing of Music: History, Method, and Practice* (Cambridge: Cambridge University Press, 1996), 82–86. See also Talle, revised preface, xxv–xxix.
4. Talle, revised preface, xxix.
5. Gerber, *Historisch-Biographisches Lexikon der Tonkünstler*, 1:76. Regarding her salary, see Wolff, *Bach: The Learned Musician*, 205. See also David, Mendel, and Wolff, *New Bach Reader*, 93–94.

6. See David Yearsley, *Sex, Death, and Minuets: Anna Magdalena and Her Musical Notebooks* (Chicago: University of Chicago Press, 2019). See also Andrew Talle, "Who Was Anna Magdalena Bach?," *BACH* 51, no. 1 (2020): 151–66.
7. Yo Tomita, "Anna Magdalena as Bach's Copyist," *Understanding Bach* 2 (2007): 71–72.
8. Talle, "Who Was Anna Magdalena Bach?," 145–46.
9. Russell Stinson, *The Bach Manuscripts of Johann Peter Kellner and His Circle: A Case Study in Reception History* (Durham, NC: Duke University Press, 1989), 14–19.
10. Stinson, *The Bach Manuscripts of Johann Peter Kellner*, 56–57. See also Talle, "Some Observations," 23–29; and Talle, revised preface, xxxi–xxxii.
11. On Kellner's miscellany volume, see Stinson, *The Bach Manuscripts of Johann Peter Kellner*, 19–30.
12. Talle, "Some Observations," 23–29.
13. Stinson, *The Bach Manuscripts of Johann Peter Kellner*, 59–60.
14. Stinson, *The Bach Manuscripts of Johann Peter Kellner*, 60–61.
15. Talle, revised preface, xxv–xxvi. See also Zoltán Szabó, "Remaining Silhouettes of Lost Bach Manuscripts? Re-evaluating J. P. Kellner's Copy of J. S. Bach's Solo String Compositions," *Understanding Bach* 10 (2015): 71–72.
16. On similar abridgements in Kellner's copy of the Violin Solos, see Talle, "Some Observations," 23–24; Stinson, *The Bach Manuscripts of Johann Peter Kellner*, 55–70; and Szabó, "Remaining Silhouettes," 78–81.
17. Ulrich Leisinger, commentary to *Suites for Violoncello Solo*, by Johann Sebastian Bach, 5th ed. (Vienna: Wiener Urtext, 2000), 2 and 6 n. 3. See also Talle, revised preface, xxvi–xxvii and xxxiv.
18. C. P. E. Bach, *Verzeichniß des musikalischen Nachlasses des verstorbenen Capellmeisters Carl Philipp Emanuel Bach* (Hamburg, 1790), 67.
19. Leisinger, commentary to *Suites for Violoncello Solo*, 7 n. 12. See also Talle, revised preface, xxvi–xxviii.
20. Leisinger, commentary to *Suites for Violoncello Solo*, 4–5. A. C. P. Bach's letters about this copyist are published in Manfred Hermann Schmid, "Das Geschäft mit dem Nachlaß von C. Ph. E. Bach," in *Carl Philipp Emanuel Bach und die europäische Musikkultur des mittleren 18. Jahrhunderts*, ed. Hans-Joachim Marx (Göttingen: Vandenhoeck & Ruprecht, 1990), 508–11.
21. See Leisinger, commentary to *Suites for Violoncello Solo*, 5. See also Talle, revised preface, xxvii. On Johann Traeg's role collecting and promoting Bach's music in Vienna, see Ulrich Leisinger, "Bachian Fugues in Mozart's Vienna," *Bach Notes: The Newsletter of the American Bach Society* 6 (Fall 2006): 1–7.

Making Sense of the Sources

22. Talle's stemmatic diagram of source relationships appears in his revised preface, xxxv.
23. Anner Bylsma, *Bach, the Fencing Master: About Mrs. Anna Magdalena Bach's Autograph Copy of the 6 Suites for Violoncello Solo senza Basso of Johann Sebastian Bach*, rev. ed. (Amsterdam: The Fencing Mail, 2019), 6.
24. Mark M. Smith, "A Deceptive Edition of the Bach 'Cello Suites," *BACH* 9, no. 1 (January 1978): 26.
25. Matt Haimovitz, *J. S. Bach: The Cello Suites According to Anna Magdalena* (Pentatone, PTC5186555, 2015).
26. For a critique of "authenticity" as a modernist musical ideology, see Richard Taruskin, *Text & Act: Essays on Music and Performance* (Oxford: Oxford University Press, 1995). On German Baroque perspectives about scores and performances, see also Stephen Rose, *Musical Authorship from Schütz to Bach* (Cambridge: Cambridge University Press, 2019), 187–212.
27. Quantz, *On Playing the Flute*, 217. Mozart, *A Treatise on the Fundamental Principles of Violin Playing*, 45 n. 1.
28. Szabó, "Precarious Presumptions," 27. See also Szabó, "Remaining Silhouettes."
29. Martin Rummel, *Bach Cello Suites: Kellner Manuscript* (Paladino Music, PMR0004, 2009).
30. Leisinger, commentary to *Suites for Violoncello Solo*, 4–6.
31. Talle, revised preface, xxxi–xxxiii. See also Talle, "Some Observations," 36–37.
32. Talle, revised preface, xxviii and xxxii.
33. Schober's copy of the Violin Solos is in a private collection.
34. Talle, revised preface, xxxvi.
35. Talle, revised preface, xxxiii.
36. The autograph of the lute version (BWV995) – the only surviving autograph material related to the Cello Suites – is catalogued as MS II.4085 at the Royal Library of Belgium. See Talle, revised preface, xviii–xvix.
37. Talle, revised preface, xxxiv.
38. Talle, revised preface, xxxiii.
39. Talle, revised preface, xxxiii.
40. Talle, revised preface, xxxvii.

4

TRANSMISSION, PERFORMANCE, AND RECEPTION: 1720–C. 1900

No figure looms larger in the reception history of Bach's Cello Suites than the Catalan cellist Pablo Casals (1876–1973). Through his recital performances, recordings, and teaching, he played a pivotal role in establishing these works as the cornerstone of the cello repertoire. Yet the mystique around Casals has tended to stave off exploration of the Cello Suites' performance history and transmission before the twentieth century.[1] To be sure, less is known about the early transmission and performance history of the Cello Suites compared to the more amply documented record for the Violin Solos.[2] Violinists Ferdinand David (1810–73) and Joseph Joachim (1831–1907) had promoted that collection to canonical status well before Casals did the same for the Cello Suites.

But, the incomplete record notwithstanding, various clues sketch out an unexpectedly robust, varied, and international performance history of the Cello Suites before the recording era. In examining this history, we retrace the steps of the first generations of musicians to grapple with such issues as tempo, dynamics, and the handling of chords as they interpreted the Cello Suites for their public concerts. A sense of the audience response to these early performances is captured in concert reviews, which ran the gamut from bewilderment and indifference toward this unusual music to unreserved praise for its expressive power.

This chapter's narrative begins by tracing how musicians began to hear *of* the Cello Suites, well before they could actually hear them in concerts. Published editions began to appear in the 1820s, the earliest among them presenting the Cello Suites as instrumental studies, with later editions being more oriented toward concert performances. The latter category included not only versions for solo cello but also editions with piano accompaniment and transcriptions for other instruments. Many of the early editions are heavily marked with added tempo markings, dynamics, and other more pronounced editorial interventions that seem misguided by today's standards. Yet these very features offer a window into understanding how the Cello Suites were played before the advent of recording.

Taken together, Chapters 4 and 5 trace 300 years of the Cello Suites' transmission, performance, and reception history. The story proceeds in a spiral, beginning in Germany in a narrow circle of musicians proximate to Bach, then expanding in the nineteenth century to early editions and performances across Western Europe (and with some outliers in Australia and the USA).[3] Through Casals's towering influence, the Cello Suites exploded in popularity and international reach throughout the twentieth century, achieving their present status as iconic works with a resonance extending well beyond the concert hall into popular culture.

Transmission of the Manuscripts: The Cello Suites' First Century

Clues about the earliest transmission of the Cello Suites (before the first editions) have already been discussed in Chapters 1 and 3; a brief summary will therefore suffice here. The surviving manuscript copies of the Cello Suites (especially Sources B, C, and D) contain markings and annotations that probably arose in the context of music making, likely during lessons or other musical interactions with the composer. Although no specific performances are documented during Bach's lifetime, there must have been ample opportunities either involving musicians of the Cöthen Capelle (possibly Abel but more likely Linike) or else within the Leipzig Collegium Musicum. Talle suggests that the manuscript belonging to C. P. E. Bach – which served as the model for Sources C and D – might have been copied in Leipzig by Johann Christoph Altnikol (1719–59), the composer's student and son-in-law, who prepared many Bach manuscripts and who, besides being a singer, violinist, and organist, was also a cellist.[4] If Talle's speculation is correct, it would be conceivable that some embellishments, articulations, and other markings preserved in

Sources C and D could have arisen through Altnikol's playing or lessons with the composer.

There is considerable evidence that Bach and his students played the Violin Solos on keyboard instruments, a practice that might have extended to the Cello Suites. A manuscript copied by Altnikol preserves keyboard transcriptions based on two of Bach's Violin Solos: The Keyboard Sonata in D Minor (BWV964) is a transcription of the Solo Violin Sonata No. 2 in A Minor (BWV1003), and the Keyboard Adagio in G (BWV968) is a transcription of the first movement of the Solo Violin Sonata No. 3 in C Major (BWV1005).[5] While it is unknown whether the composer was involved with these transcriptions,[6] Bach certainly engaged in more impromptu keyboard performances of this repertoire. His student Agricola wrote that the composer "often played [the Violin Solos] on the clavichord, adding as much in the nature of harmony as he found necessary."[7] Adlung, the Thuringian organist, likewise wrote that the Violin Solos "are actually works for violin solo *senza basso* ... though they can be played very effectively on the keyboard."[8] As noted earlier, Kellner (also a Thuringian organist) omitted information in his copy of the Cello Suites that would be essential for performances on cello, indicating that his copies of both the Violin Solos and the Cello Suites were made for playing on keyboard instruments.

Since C. P. E. Bach – the avid archivist and chronicler of his father's career – possessed a manuscript copy of the Cello Suites and commissioned the copy now known as Source C, he could have been involved with performances either in Berlin or Hamburg. His coauthored obituary of his father (written together with Agricola) highlights the Violin Solos and Cello Suites as notable instrumental works. C. P. E. Bach also furnished biographical material to Forkel, who published the first study of the elder Bach's life and works in 1802. Forkel's chapter on Bach's melody lavishes special attention on the Violin Solos and Cello Suites, marveling at the capacity of single-line instruments to express harmonically self-sufficient textures. Explaining that composers of Bach's time observed a rule that two-, three-, and four-part writing should be handled with harmony so complete that no additional voice could be added, Forkel wrote that Bach extended this principle to writing for a single part:

> To this attempt we are indebted for six solos for the violin and six others for the violoncello, which are without any accompaniment and which absolutely admit of no second singable part set to them. By particular turns in the melody, he has so combined in a single part all the notes required to make the modulation complete that a second part is neither necessary nor possible.[9]

It is unclear whether Forkel had actually seen manuscript copies of the Violin Solos or Cello Suites before he wrote these remarks, which appear to be based on earlier writings by Kirnberger: "[Compared to writing two-part duets,] it is even more difficult to write a simple melody, without the slightest accompaniment, so harmoniously that is it not possible to add a voice without mistakes. . . . In this manner, J. S. Bach wrote six sonatas for the violin and six for the violoncello, without any accompaniment."[10] Kirnberger's observations appear in an extended discussion of composition for fewer than four voices. He could have encountered the Violin Solos and/or the Cello Suites through his studies with Kellner (before 1738) or with Bach (c. 1739–41).

Forkel's comments received a rebuttal from the composer and critic Johann Friedrich Reichardt (1752–1814), who wrote that the Violin Solos and Cello Suites

> actually contain only a few such artful, completely monophonic movements in which, although one does not feel the want of a second voice, it would nevertheless often be possible [in numerous movements], even if only here and there, to add a basso continuo [*Grundbaß*], in the manner of Italian accompanying voices. Most of those movements, however, are in two, three, and sometimes even four voices. Therefore, in order to execute them, they require the highest virtuosity, precisely in the exalted sense that was sought and sometimes achieved [*gesucht und zuweilen erstrebt*] 40–50 years ago.[11]

Reichardt's reference to four-voice movements suggests that he had seen the Violin Solos either in a manuscript copy or in their first edition (published by Simrock in 1802).

The publication in 1790 of C. P. E. Bach's estate catalog, which listed the Cello Suites manuscript in his possession, spread awareness of the suites' existence and prompted the Viennese music publisher Traeg to commission the copy now known as Source

D. Traeg, in turn, listed the Cello Suites in his 1799 catalog, spreading awareness of them within Vienna's musical community.[12] Vienna at that time was home to many serious connoisseurs of Bach's music, including the noble members of the Gesellschaft der Associierten, founded by Baron Gottfried van Swieten (1733–1803), a student of Kirnberger and the dedicatee of Forkel's Bach biography. Likewise, in 1806, the estate catalog of Johann Gottfried Schwanberger (c. 1740–1804) listed the manuscript sources of the Violin Solos and Cello Suites that Anna Magdalena Bach had made for his father. That auction attracted the attention of Forkel, who purchased both manuscripts.[13]

Another notable figure in the Cello Suites' early transmission is the organist, composer, and cellist Ernst Ludwig Gerber (1746–1819), who was a prominent music collector and lexicographer. The son of Bach's student Heinrich Nicolaus Gerber (1702–75), he compiled an encyclopedia of composers (published 1790–92) that contained an article on Bach with a works list including "six sonatas for violin without bass" and "six of the same for cello,"[14] echoing language found in the obituary by Agricola and C. P. E. Bach. In the revised works list included in the lexicon's expanded edition (1812–14), he listed "six suites for cello, without accompaniment,"[15] curiously omitting the Violin Solos. Gerber's switch in designation from "sonatas" to "suites" suggests that, in the intervening years between the two editions of his lexicon, he consulted either C. P. E. Bach's estate catalog or else perhaps some manuscript copy that bore the title "suites."

Since Gerber performed as a cellist in public concerts in Leipzig c. 1765–75 – and considering his connections to musicians in Bach's circle and his penchant for collecting scores – it is conceivable that he might somehow have seen a manuscript copy of the Cello Suites. Gerber's lexicon became the source material for articles about Bach in two early nineteenth-century music dictionaries published respectively in France and England.[16] The latter describes the Violin Solos as "a most unique work" and refers to the Cello Suites as being "similar" to the Violin Solos.[17]

The First Editions: c. 1824–1826

About a century after the Cello Suites were composed, the first printed editions appeared in the mid 1820s. These editions presented the Cello Suites primarily as exercises, a conception reflecting the proliferation of instrumental études for use at music conservatories after 1800. As a point of comparison, a lauding overview of Bach's music by the Parisian pianist and music critic Amédée Méreaux (1802–74) characterizes the composer's keyboard suites as "true studies of technique [*mécanisme*]."[18] Given the obscure status of the German Baroque solo-violin tradition, many nineteenth-century musicians lacked a context to understand the Violin Solos or Cello Suites as concert music and must have considered them to be curiosities that somewhat resembled instrumental études.

The first edition of the Cello Suites, titled *Six Sonates ou études pour le violoncelle composées par J. Sébastien Bach, œuvre posthume*, was published in 1824 at the initiative of the Parisian cellist Louis-Pierre Norblin (1781–1854).[19] An editorial preface ("Avis des éditeurs") outlines the edition's rationale as follows: Together with Bach's "fugues for the piano" and "études for the violin," the Cello Suites would "complete a course of exercises for the three principal instruments of modern music" – a course that had been stymied by the lack of an edition or accessible manuscript source for the Cello Suites. However, the preface continues, "after extensive research in Germany, Mr. Norblin ... finally reaped the fruit of his perseverance by discovering this precious manuscript."[20] Although the preface acknowledges Norblin as having located the manuscript source for the edition, he is not explicitly identified as editor.

Norblin evidently went to considerable effort to identify a manuscript on which to base his edition. The manuscript in question was either the one that had belonged to C. P. E. Bach or else a copy based on it, given various similarities between the articulation marks (strokes) in Norblin's edition and those in Sources C and D (which were also based on that same manuscript).[21] Another similarity between Norblin's edition and Source C is the atypical notation of the C minor key signature for Suite No. 5 – with three flats plus one natural on the staff's top line – to indicate

Example 4.1 Suite No. 1 in G Major, Gigue, syncopated ties as edited by Louis-Pierre Norblin. Reproduced by permission of the Music and Theater Library of Sweden.

that the key signature's A♭ should not be applied to the *scordatura* top string.

However, Norblin added many indications that are original to his edition, such as tempo markings, fingerings, and some occasional dynamics. The edition is riddled with erroneous notes and titles, such as substituting "corrente" for all six "courantes" and (more egregiously) "loure" for the Bourrées of Suites Nos. 3–4, a designation that would be copied in many subsequent editions. Another influential eccentricity is the introduction of syncopated ties in the Gigue from Suite No. 1 on each statement of the principal motive (see Example 4.1). These ties were repeated in many editions and influenced performances and recordings for well over a century, including those by Casals. Bowings are indicated through slur markings, but no directional bow markings (∨ or ⊓) are included, a choice that set the standard for most subsequent editions.

The edition's title (*Six Sonates ou études* [. . .]) is curious given that Norblin's manuscript source identified the collection as "suites." Perhaps Norblin (or his publisher) might have considered "sonatas" to be more marketable than the outmoded genre of "suites." Whatever the reason for the volume's title, its editorial preface does, in fact, alternate between the terms "études" and "suites":

> This collection is composed of six suites, each divided in six pieces. The sixth suite is the only one devoted to the high register of the violoncello. The rest of the work is designed to exercise the low positions. Since the true character of the instrument is found in the low register, that is where the real difficulties [*les difficultés les plus réelles*] are found. Therefore, Bach's études for the violoncello

The First Editions: c. 1824–1826

will be no less timeless [*classiques*] than his other works, and the publication of this collection is bound to be a great success. In making it known, we believe we are doing a service to amateurs and professionals of this instrument, to all friends of good music, and to the entire art form.

Regarding the high tessitura of Suite No. 6, although Norblin's manuscript source included the indication "à cinque cordes," instructing the player to use a five-string instrument, Norblin omits that information from his edition. Since by the 1820s virtually no cellists used five-string instruments, Norblin's edition tacitly assumes that Suite No. 6 will be executed on a standard, four-string cello. This option – which to this day remains the most common way to perform Suite No. 6 – requires the player to become fluent in the highest reaches of the cello fingerboard, posing extreme technical challenges even for highly capable players. Norblin's fingerings, therefore, represent the first documentation of a cellist grappling with the considerable difficulties posed by performing Suite No. 6 on a four-string instrument. If Norblin understood the Cello Suites as études aspiring toward total mastery of the cello, then Suite No. 6 (as performed on a four-string cello) would represent a crowning achievement of a virtuoso player. Although some later editions would include indications that Suite No. 6 had been composed for a five-string cello, it is unclear if any cellist ever performed it on such an instrument before the turn of the twentieth century (see Chapter 5).

Around the time his edition appeared, Norblin took up an appointment as cello professor at the Paris Conservatoire (serving 1824–41), where he was an influential teacher and figured prominently in Parisian concert life.[22] Nevertheless, there is no record indicating that the Cello Suites found a new Parisian audience through his or his students' performances. Moreover, his edition did not circulate widely; only one exemplar is known to survive today.[23] Nor does his edition appear to have influenced the cello curriculum at the Paris Conservatoire, judging from the preface to the cello method of Bernhard Romberg (1767–1841).[24] Despite the edition's small circulation, it was nevertheless included in an 1825 list of newly published music that appeared in a Parisian journal.[25]

The second edition, published in Leipzig c. 1825 by Heinrich Albert Probst (1791–1846), is essentially a reprint of the Paris edition, closely mirroring its text as well as the orthography of the title page.[26] The editorial preface is omitted, and no editor is credited, making this edition a second version of Norblin's original. The Probst edition circulated more widely than Norblin's, serving as the basis for other reprint editions. Until recently, it was often misidentified as the earliest edition.[27]

Around 1826, Justus Johann Friedrich Dotzauer (1783–1860) published a new, corrected edition with Breitkopf & Härtel in Leipzig under the title *Six Solos ou études pour le violoncelle, ouvrage posthume*. Based partly on the earlier editions (probably Probst specifically), Dotzauer incorporated extensive corrections based on some other manuscript source.[28] These revisions largely involved simplifying or removing Norblin's performance indications, fingerings, and ornaments, making his a considerably cleaner edition. The only added dynamic markings are in the Prelude to Suite No. 6, where Dotzauer continues the echo effects systematically throughout. He also significantly revised the slur markings, based partly on his manuscript source and partly on his instincts as a cellist. His bowing preferences tend toward smoothing out articulations by lengthening slurs as well as toward applying slurs more consistently to repeated figurations throughout a movement.[29] Dotzauer's fingering choices in some passages reflect his fondness for slides (*portamento*) to the upper positions on the middle strings, anticipating expressive effects and distinctive colors that would be explored more fully in editions from the second half of the century (see Example 4.2).[30] Dotzauer considered the upper positions of the D string to have a characteristically honeyed or sweet sound (*son moelleux*).[31]

As in Norblin's edition, the individual suites are designated Sonata I, Sonata II, and so on. His tempo designations are largely similar or identical to Norblin's, with the notable exception of the Prelude to Suite No. 3; where Norblin's edition indicates "Allegro," Dotzauer's has "Presto," preserving one of the few tempo markings likely present in his manuscript source. Since the "presto" marking also appears in Kellner's manuscript copy (Source B), it is reasonable to conclude that this marking was present in Dotzauer's

Example 4.2 Justus Johann Friedrich Dotzauer, two passages marked with *portamento* fingerings.
  a. Suite No. 1 in G Major, Menuet II.
  b. Suite No. 2 in D Minor, Sarabande.

manuscript source, which belongs to the same branch of the Cello Suites' stemmatic tree.[32] Dotzauer also corrected some of Norblin's movement titles, indicating "courante" (where Norblin has "corrente") and "bourrée" (where Norblin has "loure"). In the Gavotte II from Suite No. 6, he adds the title "La Mussette [*sic*]" in recognition of the section with a prominent D-string drone.

The principal cellist of the Dresden Court Orchestra (1821–50), Dotzauer was an influential performer and pedagogue associated with the Dresden school of cello performance.[33] Although his edition of the Cello Suites was initially overlooked in German reviews of Dotzauer's other cello publications,[34] the edition eventually circulated widely in many reprints and remained in use well into the twentieth century. An 1893 survey of cello music listed Dotzauer's edition of the Cello Suites under "Exercises," describing them as "difficult, but extremely interesting and perhaps the most useful study in the whole of the violoncello literature."[35] Dotzauer's edition was also listed in Franz Pazdírek's c. 1904 catalog of printed music.[36]

Although the editions discussed so far present the Cello Suites as études to cultivate instrumental mastery, at least one author familiar with Dotzauer's edition considered them to be suitable for concerts or church settings:

It was the custom in the time of Bach, on festivals and before the communion, to perform a solo or concert upon some instrument; hence there are few instruments for which he has not written some composition. It was to this custom that, in all probability, we owe the origin of the celebrated solos for the violin and violoncello; the latter, we understand, have been recently published by Dotzauer.[37]

The fleeting mention in this 1838 review of various Bach editions is virtually the only early published reference to Dotzauer's edition of the Cello Suites. The critic had most likely not seen the edition, judging from the wording of his remarks and the fact that it is not included in the list of thirty items under review.

That the first generation of editions presented Bach's Cello Suites as pedagogical material explains the lack of known public performances during the first half of the nineteenth century. A record of performances of individual movements and some complete suites starting around 1860 reflects several factors, including the cultural influence of the Bach revival, the growing profile of the Violin Solos, and the rise of a generation of internationally touring cello soloists.

Piano Accompaniments and Transcriptions: 1853–1893

One trend that helped to usher both the Violin Solos and the Cello Suites into the concert hall was the tradition of performing with added piano accompaniment.[38] The perceived need for such accompaniment stems from the then-widespread view that compositions for unaccompanied violin or cello were essentially technical studies lacking audience appeal. The following comments by the American composer Edgar Stillman Kelley (1857–1944) are symptomatic. In an article about accompaniments for the Cello Suites by Robert Schumann (1810–56) (discussed later in this chapter), Kelley described what he regarded as the deficits of the unaccompanied version: "The second number [of Suite No. 1] is an Allemande, which, in its original form, is the least interesting of the entire suite, being for the most part a series of scale passages with an occasional arpeggio and now and then a trill."[39] Kelley apparently believed that Bach's music tended to garner respect more than genuine fondness:

I remember particularly one occasion when I tried a peculiar experiment. At a reception given by one of the leading artists in San Francisco [around 1883]

Piano Accompaniments and Transcriptions: 1853–1893

a number of young gentlemen and ladies wished to dance the Sir Roger de Coverly. Knowing the awe in which many of them held the fugue writer, I volunteered to play for the dance, making use of the gigue from the 'cello suite [No. 1], and while they thoroughly enjoyed the music, they were still more elated to learn afterwards that they had heard something by Bach which they could appreciate on the first hearing.[40]

Another middling appraisal of the Cello Suites appeared in a review of a performance by Alfredo Piatti (1822–1901) of a prelude, courante, and allemande at London's Monday Popular Concerts in 1868:

Compared with the six sonatas for violin without accompaniment these violoncello solos are light and unpretending. Nevertheless, they are interesting, if only because they are Bach's. The first and last (in C major) are little better than exercises for the acquirement of mechanical facility, more suitable to the studio than to the concert-room, for which they were clearly never intended; but the second (in G minor [sic]) is melodious and replete with sentiment.[41]

Despite the mixed opinion of the Cello Suites as concert repertoire, the reviewer nevertheless had unalloyed praise for Piatti's performance: "In what masterly style they were executed by Signor Piatti will easily be understood: tone, phrasing, accent, manipulation more absolutely perfect could not well be imagined.... This gentleman is conspicuous as the greatest of living professors of his instrument."[42]

A more scathing rebuke comes from the organist Charles Maclean (1843–1916), whose rave review of a 1904 performance by cellist Julius Klengel (1859–1933) is interrupted by a ranting tangent about the unsuitability of the Violin Solos for concert performances:

Julius Klengel's tour de force, Bach's No. 5 Suite in C minor for violoncello solo, was wholly astonishing. Those dreary violin solos (a twelfth higher), with the performer struggling with four-part chords which exasperatingly upset the rhythm at every other bar, are known to patient concert goers, and it is a pity they ever leave the class-room. Here there was no such sense, and perhaps Klengel also had a rather flat bridge. He gave twenty minutes of this without a flaw of intonation, and one would not have wished it a minute shorter.[43]

For those who regarded solo-string music as études or compositional curiosities, Elizabeth Field writes, "added piano accompaniments [served] to turn them into 'serious' music."[44] Piano accompaniments for the Cello Suites were prepared by Schumann, Friedrich Wilhelm Stade (1817–1902), and Carl Grädener (1812–83), among others.[45] Schumann, who had become deeply engaged with Bach's music, was initially drawn to compose accompaniments for the Violin Solos because he "found a quantity of pieces which would be considerably improved by a piano accompaniment and thus accessible to a larger public."[46] He soon turned to what he called Bach's "cello sonatas," which he deemed "the most beautiful and important compositions ever written for violoncello."[47]

Robert Schumann and Clara Schumann (1819–96) tried out the new accompaniments in a private reading with cellist Christian Reimers (1827–89) over two days at New Year's 1853–54, marking the first known occasion in which a cellist played all six suites.[48] Regrettably, Schumann never succeeded in finding a publisher for his accompaniments. His 1853 manuscript is now lost, and the only known surviving source is a manuscript copy of Suite No. 3 written by cellist Julius Goltermann (1823–76). Copies of Schumann's arrangement circulated enough to facilitate at least two performances: an 1879 performance of Suite No. 1 in Stuttgart, by Julius Cabisius (1841–98) with pianist Dionys Pruckner (1834–96), and an 1884 performance of the Gavottes from Suite No. 6 in Adelaide, by Reimers (who had settled there) with pianist Gotthold Reimann (1859–1932).[49] Kelley, who was Cabisius's housemate, regularly played Schumann's accompaniment to Suite No. 1 with him privately, and his article preserves several short excerpts.[50]

Stade's 1864 edition is not only the first published arrangement with piano accompaniment but also the third novel edition of any kind (after those by Norblin/Probst and Dotzauer). The detailed fingerings and bowing instructions in the cello part suggest that Stade – who was not a cellist – must have collaborated with some uncredited cellist colleague.[51] Stade's edition was also published with a viola part – identical to the cello version but transposed an octave higher and lacking any bowings or fingerings – making it the earliest known edition for viola.[52] The absence of performance indications in the viola part indicate that it was prepared mechanically, with very little care. Some passages in Suite No. 6 are nearly unplayable as presented, without any editorial fingerings to suggests how a violist might navigate the passagework in high positions or play such awkward chords as $d'–a'–f\sharp''$. Two public, non-cello performances of Stade's arrangement took place at his initiative at concerts of the Altenburg Singakademie. An 1869 performance of the Sarabande from Suite No. 4 on trombone with organ received a positive review: "[The trombonist's playing] contained not only power and force, but also a rare softness and songful lyricism of tone."[53] One year later, a viola performance of Suite No. 1 with organ accompaniment likewise made a "magnificent impression," according to a reviewer, who adds that "the elegiac tone of the viola combines even better with that of the organ than the cello could."[54]

Where Schumann's accompaniment tends toward simple, block chords, Stade's and Grädener's are at times more elaborate, with varied figurations, textures, articulations, and dynamics. Notwithstanding Kelley's opinion that Schumann "undoubtedly was seeking to harmonize the work as much as possible in the spirit of Bach" or Grädener's stated intention to "match as much as possible to Bach's intentions,"[55] all three of these piano accompaniments are thoroughly rooted in Romantic aesthetics and compositional practices, bearing little resemblance to a version Bach himself might have conceived.[56]

The practice of performing the Cello Suites with piano accompaniment persisted until the early decades of the twentieth century. David Popper (1843–1913) performed an (unspecified) Bach sarabande with piano accompaniment "with excellent mastery" at an 1864 concert in Leipzig.[57] Piatti performed various combinations of movements – sometimes from different suites – in many concerts from 1859 to 1873, including a critically acclaimed 1873 performance of "a *Suite de pieces* in G major, by Bach," probably referring to the complete Suite No. 1.[58] His performances of the same suite in 1892–93, with his own piano accompaniment, received more mixed reviews. Piatti's student William Whitehouse (1859–1935) explained that Piatti had composed accompaniments for all six suites, "but the appearance of the first of these in G was met with such indignation and abuse that he would not have the others printed."[59] An aside in Whitehouse's memoirs suggests that some nineteenth-century musicians were familiar with Bach's practice of playing his Violin Solos at the keyboard:

> I once asked Joachim why Schumann wrote such ornate and over-elaborate pianoforte accompaniments to the Sonatas for violin alone of Bach. His reply was that he (Schumann) wrote them "as a task or exercise." ... He went on to say that he believed Bach wrote these wonderful Sonatas very rapidly, perhaps one in a couple of days! Tried it over with a fine violinist friend, and played it at night at some distinguished patron's house in a music-room built for camera music – and *Bach* would himself sit at the harpsichord and *fill in a slight accompaniment*![60]

At least one reviewer took kindly to Piatti's cello-piano version: "There is little authority for such an addition [of piano accompaniment], but the improvement in the effect is undeniable."[61]

In 1870, a critic compared two interpretations of the same unspecified Bach gavotte, both in Leipzig during the same season, the first played unaccompanied by Jules de Swert (1843–91) and the second performed by Friedrich Grützmacher (1832–1903) with piano: "Mr. Grützmacher was at his best in the pieces Air and Gavotte by J. S. Bach. The latter would have been even more effective without piano accompaniment and we remember that Mr. J. de Swert played the same piece without accompaniment in the second Gewandhaus Concert and with great success."[62] The latter part of the nineteenth century evidently saw changing tastes and practices around the use of piano accompaniment for the Cello Suites.

These same decades also saw the publication of transcriptions of the Cello Suites for violin, piano, and other instruments. Ferdinand David, concertmaster at the Leipzig Gewandhaus, published a violin transcription around 1866 intended for students at the Leipzig Conservatory to use as preparatory studies before undertaking the Violin Solos.[63] In his edition, which includes a piano accompaniment by Friedrich Hermann (1828–1907), David shortens the bass notes in some chords or else indicates that they should be rolled before the beat, thereby encouraging violinists to prioritize the sustained melody. Such rhythmic modification appears in several sarabandes, the Menuet from Suite No. 2, the "Loure II" from Suite No. 4, and several movements from Suite No. 5.

Piano Accompaniments and Transcriptions: 1853–1893

In a rare public performance of the Cello Suites on violin, David played three movements from Suite No. 5 (Prelude, Sarabande, and Gavottes) at the Leipzig Gewandhaus for a New Year's concert in 1865. An enthusiastic American critic wrote that whichever publisher would release David's then-in-progress edition "must not approach them as mere mechanical studies – they are true poems."[64] The influential Leipzig critic Yourij von Arnold (1811–98) was less impressed, holding that the Cello Suites "can arouse no great interest (unless it were historical)."[65]

Over the ensuing century, various transcriptions – often of individual movements from the Cello Suites – were created with a similarly pedagogical aim. The earliest known double-bass transcription also appeared toward the end of the century, according to an 1896 list of newly published string music that includes "*Four Suites*, Op. 50 from the six suites for violoncello, by Joh. Seb. Bach, edited and fingered for the double bass, by Otto Stex."[66] Perhaps the most ubiquitous violin arrangements are the four pieces adapted from the Cello Suites for the violin method of Suzuki Shin'ichi (1898–1998). Starting in the decades after World War II, hundreds of thousands of violin students in Japan, the United States, and elsewhere have used these method books, representing perhaps the largest cohort of students learning music adapted from Bach's Cello Suites. In the 1920s, Suzuki had studied violin in Berlin with Karl Klingler (1879–1971), a student and close friend of Joachim, who was in turn a student of David. It is therefore probable that Suzuki's view of Cello Suite movements as appropriate pedagogical material for developing violinists was influenced by a German tradition stemming from David.

Various solo-piano transcriptions based on the Violin Solos and Cello Suites also appeared starting in the 1860s. The best known of these transcriptions was by Joachim Raff (1822–82), whose solo-piano edition includes the complete Cello Suites richly annotated with editorial dynamics and articulations reflecting nineteenth-century performance style.[67] Several pianists, among them Agnes Zimmermann (1847–1925) and Sara Heinze (1837–1901), also published solo-piano transcriptions of individual movements intended for students; Heinze's transcriptions of four movements

95

are included in her compilation of Bach's keyboard music for student pianists, which was frequently reprinted as late as 1958.[68] A piano transcription of the Courante from Suite No. 3 by Noël Desjoyeaux (1861–1947) was offered in 1904 as a "musical supplement" gifted to subscribers of the influential French music journal *Le Ménestrel*.[69]

Critics reviewing the various solo-piano versions often noted the obscurity of the Cello Suites. One commented that piano transcriptions offered "a charmingly quaint piece of music ... rescued from the oblivion of Bach's violoncello sonatas and made generally accessible."[70] Another reviewer – discussing an edition of six movements arranged for elementary pianists – expressed his perception that, at the time of his writing in 1892, the Cello Suites had been played more widely in various piano transcriptions than in the original: "It is but natural that the [cello] suites of Bach, which are heard so seldom on the instrument for which they were written by the illustrious and immortal composer, and have been arranged [for piano] in different ways (difficult and very difficult), should also be presented in an easy manner."[71]

The Next Solo-Cello Editions: 1866–1900

Grützmacher – a "grand-student" of Dotzauer and colleague of David at the Leipzig Gewandhaus and Leipzig Conservatory – published two distinct editions in short succession: his "concert" edition (c. 1866) and the "original" edition (c. 1867).[72] The latter is the more conservative edition, presenting the basic text of the suites with added tempo designations, dynamics, articulations, bowings, fingerings, and occasional other expressive markings. The main textual deviation from earlier editions pertains to the treatment of chords. As in David's violin transcription, Grützmacher renotates many chords so that bass notes are either shortened or given as grace notes, implying that they should be played before the beat and that the cellist should emphasize the sustained melody (see Example 4.3).

Grützmacher's concert edition, on the other hand, takes such extravagant liberties as to seem more like an interpretive paraphrase than a traditional edition. For its departure from modern editorial

The Next Solo-Cello Editions: 1866–1900

Example 4.3 Chords as renotated in Friedrich Grützmacher's "original" edition.
   a. Suite No. 1 in G Major, Sarabande.
   b. Suite No. 5 in C Minor, Allemande.
   c. Suite No. 6 in D Major, Sarabande.

practices and cello techniques, his concert edition has been judged harshly in recent scholarship. One of the more mildly worded critiques describes it as "Grützmacher's most unforgivable contribution" in which "he completely reorganized [the Cello Suites] with additional chords and embellishments, so presenting a travesty of the composer's work."[73]

In a similar vein to piano transcriptions and paraphrases by Franz Liszt (1811–86) based on symphonic, operatic, and art-song repertoires, Grützmacher's concert edition represents a free, creative transformation of its source, refracted through the musical imagination and instrumental idiom of a particular virtuoso. Grützmacher's concert version liberally adds chords to flesh out or intensify the harmonies and to reinforce metrical accents. Other recompositions include new patterns of figuration in the Preludes to Suites Nos. 1 and 4 and the introduction of syncopated accents and other metrical dissonances in many passages of the Courante from Suite No. 3 (see Example 4.4). Suite No. 6 is transposed down a fifth to G major, presumably because the lower tessitura facilitates added chords.

The concert edition is also dense with expressive markings and performance indications, including various then-modern cellistic techniques such as expressive *portamento* (indicated "gliss." in the Menuet of Suite No. 1, the Allemandes of Suites Nos. 5 and 6, and the Gavotte I of Suite No. 6), flying staccato (indicated by a slur with dots, found extensively in scalar passages of the Prelude to Suite No. 3), and coloristic fingerings in uncommonly high positions (as in the Gavotte II from Suite No. 5). As in the original edition, the bass notes of many chords are shortened or rendered as grace notes. Overall, this version suggests the expressive intensity and supreme virtuosity that Grützmacher must have exuded in his bravura performances.[74]

Grützmacher was probably among the first cellists to program complete suites regularly.[75] His free approach to editing was not unique to his concert edition of the Cello Suites.[76] Indeed, when his publisher rejected an edition that he had prepared of Schumann's cello music, he responded with a heated letter defending his editorial philosophy in general and its validity for the Cello Suites in particular:

> My main purpose has been to reflect and to determine what these masters might have been thinking, and to set down all that they, themselves, could have indicated. ... I feel *I have more right than all the others to do this work*. ...

The Next Solo-Cello Editions: 1866–1900

Example 4.4 Suite No. 1 in G Major, Courante, comparing Friedrich Grützmacher's "concert" and "original" editions.

My concert version of the Bach Suites, which you likewise mention, cannot also be a subject of reproach since, in editing them, I not only tried to follow the *same intentions* of which I have just spoken, but I succeeded in it. I have reaped much success in presenting this edition in concert, something that would have been impossible with the bare original in its primitive state.[77]

If Grützmacher's concert edition represents an extreme instance of flamboyant editorial intervention (bordering on recomposition or paraphrase), the polar opposite would be the 1877 Bach-Gesellschaft edition edited by Alfred Dörffel (1821–1905).[78] The Bach-Gesellschaft was founded in 1850 with a mandate to

Example 4.4 (Cont.)

publish Bach's complete works without editorial interventions. Dörffel's is the first of many editions based primarily on a comparative study of the available manuscript sources, especially Anna Magdalena Bach's copy (Source A), with virtually no performance indications besides slurs, trills, and a handful of staccato dots found in the manuscript sources. It is one of the first editions to show the Gigue from Suite No. 1 without the syncopated ties introduced by Norblin (see Example 4.1). The earliest edition to omit the syncopated ties in the Gigue from Suite No. 1 is Grädener's 1871 version with piano accompaniment, where the movement is marked "leggiero" in the cello part. Even after the authoritative Bach-Gesellschaft edition

The Next Solo-Cello Editions: 1866–1900

Example 4.5 Suite No. 1 in G Major, Prelude, as edited by Hugo Becker. Reproduced by permission of McGill University.

removed the ties, they nevertheless appeared in some later editions. Evidently, they had become traditional, and many performers continued to play them well into the twentieth century. Dörffel also gives the correct title for the bourrée movements, which had been erroneously designated "loure" in many editions.

Although the Bach-Gesellschaft's hefty tomes were conceived as scholarly editions, their austere, source-based approach influenced performance editions. An 1891 edition by Robert Hausmann (1852–1909), for example, explicitly identifies its manuscript and printed sources and minimizes editorial intervention. A member of the Joachim Quartet and close associate of Johannes Brahms (1833–97), Hausmann created the most conservative edition produced by a cellist, essentially representing a "playable" version of the Bach-Gesellschaft text, adding only minor performance suggestions – articulations, metronome indications, fingerings, and some dynamics to extend the echo effects in the Prelude to Suite No. 6. Hausmann provides two versions of Suite No. 5: one showing the original *scordatura* notation and another altered to be playable in standard tuning.

Other editions of the same generation – such as those by Klengel and by Hugo Becker (1863–1941) – include somewhat more by way of performance indications and other editorial suggestions, but overall they reflect this more restrained editorial approach, with fingerings that are practical rather than indicative of expressive effects.[79] A student of both Piatti and Grützmacher, Becker's most significant innovation is the legato performance of the Prelude to Suite No. 1, an interpretive choice that influenced cellists for many decades, notably including Casals (see Example 4.5).

Even as the later nineteenth century saw the Cello Suites increasingly played in concert halls by world-class performers, they also remained in use as teaching material to cultivate or test a student cellist's mastery of the instrument. In 1881, the Metropolitan Examinations sponsored by London's Royal Academy of Music required cellists to perform a movement from the Cello Suites.[80] Whitehouse recounts playing the Prelude from Suite No. 3 at the Royal Academy of Music at a competition judged by Joachim during the same year.[81] The Paris Conservatoire regularly adopted the Cello Suites for their annual *concours* beginning in 1909. In that year, *Le Ménestrel* reported on a dozen student performances of the Sarabande from Suite No. 2, describing one *premier prix* winner's performance as a "very good sarabande but with too much vibrato" and another as possessing "bravura [*crânerie*], color, élan; also a few imprecise details and sometimes a little harshness, but a true temperament."[82]

The foregoing discussion has focused on England and especially Germany, where many performances took place and where all important nineteenth-century editions of the Cello Suites were published. However, numerous performances took place in France and Belgium during the later nineteenth century, some by internationally known cellists, and apparently rarely with accompaniment. A casual perusal of the French musical press may be misleading, however, as the numerous references to cellists performing "the prelude by Bach" – especially when accompanied by organ or harmonium – refer not to the Cello Suites but to the enormously popular *Méditation sur le premier prelude de Piano de S. Bach* (1853), today better known as "Ave Maria," by Charles Gounod (1818–93). References to the "air for the violoncello from Bach's *Suite in D*" have likewise been mistaken as indicating *Cello* Suite No. 6 when they actually refer to the celebrated movement from *Orchestral* Suite No. 3 (BWV 1068).[83]

In 1863, the cellist Henry-Marie-Joseph Poëncet (1834–73) performed "one of the small suites of J. S. Bach, in D major" – the complete Suite No. 6? – as an entr'acte within a Pasdeloup Orchestra *Concerts populaires* program consisting mostly of symphonies.[84] An 1866 chamber music concert at the Lycée Louis-le-Grand included a performance of an unspecified Bach sarabande played "with great sensitivity" by the German cellist Wilhelm Müller (1834–97).[85] In the same year, Hans von Bülow

The Next Solo-Cello Editions: 1866–1900

(1830–94) organized a chamber music concert at the Salle de la Bourse featuring musicians from the Basel Symphony Orchestra, with a program including the Sarabande, Menuets, and Courante from Suite No. 1.[86] Beyond these Parisian venues, chamber music concerts at the fashionable Casino Gassion, situated in the Pyrenean commune of Pau, included performances by cellist Édouard-André Harndorff (1846–after 1887) of an unspecified Bach sarabande and gavotte on at least two occasions, in 1879 and 1881.[87] The Belgian cello prodigy Marix Loevensohn (1880–1943) – later solo cellist of the Concertgebouw Orchestra and a prominent chamber musician – gave a critically acclaimed 1897 recital in Brussels that included an unspecified Bach gavotte.[88]

The Parisian musician who most frequently performed music from the Cello Suites was Jules Delsart (1844–1900), a cellist and viol player associated with the Paris Conservatoire and the Société des instruments anciens. Delsart regularly played individual movements from the Cello Suites in concerts from around 1868 until 1882, including multiple performances of an unspecified "Gavotte by Bach, for violoncello and orchestra."[89] After 1900, Parisian performances of individual movements or increasingly of complete suites became commonplace, especially in concerts organized by the Société J.-S. Bach that featured various cellists including Casals.[90]

Although we can only speculate about what performances of the Cello Suites before the recording era actually sounded like, they must have fallen on a spectrum – like the editions – from more expressive to more restrained. Succinct concert reviews in nineteenth-century journals generally lack details about performance style, typically commenting on the (still obscure) pieces, the overall quality of a cellist's playing, and the audience response. A critic reviewing a performance by Heinrich Wohlers (c. 1821–80) of two movements from Suite No. 6 reported simply that the cellist "played the Sarabande and Gavotte (*la Musette*) for cello by S. Bach very commendably."[91] A performance by Grützmacher – presumably of his indulgent concert version – elicited only the following terse report: "A quartet by L. Hoffmann was followed by a Suite for Cello by J. S. Bach, which gave

Mr. Grützmacher the opportunity to present his eminent technique in the brightest light."[92] Yet other critics were positively ebullient:

> Mr. F. Grützmacher from Dresden aroused a veritable storm of applause with his performance of Bach's suite for violoncello solo. ... One simply did not know what to admire more: old Bach's truly inexhaustible gift of invention and combination, which constantly reveals the new and the surprising, and which here, despite such an extraordinarily limited medium, was nevertheless able to offer such a wealth of varied and interesting ideas; or the performance style – clear and correct, extremely refined, suffused with intelligence, meticulously worked out unto the finest detail – which so completely adapted and subordinated itself to Bach's spirit, while at the same time, with great skill and the finest artistic understanding, employing the means gained in modern technique to serve that same spirit, and thus brought the whole a good deal closer to the artistic consciousness of the present day through a treatment that was as intellectual as it was discreet in every respect.[93]

Occasionally, critics offered more nuance about the interpretation, as in the following review of an 1865 performance by Louis Lübeck (1838–1904), which contrasts the special qualities of his sarabande to his dryer, perfunctory approach to other movements:

> Mr. Lübeck performed three violoncello pieces by Seb. Bach clearly and correctly. However, it was not until the Sarabande – which, in contrast to the proud character of this Spanish national dance, was much closer to our [German] way of feeling and of looking at things due to its almost modern, rapturously elegiac and soulful melody – that he succeeded in achieving a deeper and more emotional involvement [with the music] and greater warmth of tone to a highly commendable degree, which the audience appreciated through rich applause.[94]

Hugo Wolf (1860–1903) minced no words in his cutting review of an 1886 recital by Hausmann. A fervent Wagnerian, Wolf cared for neither Hausmann's sober playing style nor his conservative recital program:

> We can attest to having seldom heard so mediocre a cellist. Herr Hausmann's playing was as cold and contrived as the compositions he played, and as boring too. ... May a Bach sarabande and bourrée excite visions and the sound of angel voices; may one be a lunatic and find a redeeming world-riddle behind every note from the pen of the great Bach.[95]

Becker, writing several decades later in his cello treatise of 1929, complained of a sentimental, emotionally charged style of

Example 4.6 Suite No. 6 in D Major, Gavotte II, as arranged by W. H. Squire.

Bach performance, railing specifically against the continuous vibrato that was increasingly in vogue among a younger generation of players:

> Also in the performance of Bach's music vibrato should only be used discreetly. But how is it ordered nowadays? The whining, effeminate Bach playing of many over-sensitive cellists often has an intolerable effect. Serious classical music cannot bear any erotic vibrato; it needs a feeling for style, nobility, and dignity, without any loss of warmth. It is a sign of the weakness of a performing artist if his means of expression in vibrato are exhausted.[96]

Although these remarks appear specifically within a discussion of vibrato, they nevertheless paint a clear picture of an Apollonian ideal in Bach performance, as a foil to the "over-sensitive" interpretations that Becker disdained. Evoking unsettling, fascist overtones about degeneracy and effeminacy in musical performance, Becker's comments seem at odds with his own edition, which is replete with markings calling for expressive effects. For instance, in the Menuet II of Suite No. 1, he indicates many dynamic nuances, the coloristic use of high position and natural harmonics, and *portato* articulation.

Some musicians brought a lighter touch to the galanteries, which afforded a contrast with the more serious preceding sarabandes. Cellist William Henry Squire (1871–1963) invoked a humorous effect in his cello-piano arrangement of the Gavotte II from Suite No. 6, combining an exaggerated *glissando* effect (descending a major sixth to the open A string) with a syncopated *sforzando* (see Example 4.6). The playful character suggested by Squire's markings may relate to that movement's traditional nickname, "la Musette," as indicated in editions such as Dotzauer's and Stade's and reflecting its rustic elements. Both of Grützmacher's editions likewise designate this Gavotte II as "scherzando." Squire probably adopted the syncopated *sforzando* based on Becker's edition, which has a similar marking but without the *glissando*. George Kennaway, an expert in the history of cello playing, observes that this gesture in Squire's arrangement resembles similar *portamenti* in (non-Bach) gavottes as recorded by both Becker and Casals.[97] Even Hausmann's conservative edition hints at a contrast of character by calling for a significant tempo change between the two gavottes ($\quarternote$ =72 for Gavotte I vs. a sprightlier $\quarternote$ =96 for Gavotte II), departing from his typical practice of keeping the same tempo for pairs of galanteries. Richard Taruskin characterizes Casals's recordings of all galanteries (minuets, bourrées, and gavottes) as "Jovian scherzos."[98]

Among the cellists who produced the editions surveyed in this chapter, only Klengel's interpretation of this repertoire is captured on record: a c. 1927 studio recording of the Sarabande from Suite No. 6, played in Stade's cello-piano arrangement (i.e., not the solo-cello version found in Klengel's own edition).[99] Recorded when the cellist was nearly seventy years old, his playing encapsulates many features of the previous century's performance traditions: seamless phrasing betraying an aesthetic of "endless melody," pronounced *portamenti* (slides) on all slurred melodic leaps in both directions, narrow vibrato used almost continuously on long notes, a grand *ritardando* at the movement's close, and of course the piano accompaniment. A *Gramophone* critic found the piano accompaniment "well done and surely preferable to listening to the 'cello struggling with three- and four-part harmony."[100]

Many of these same elements are present in recordings made in 1920 by a younger British cellist, Beatrice Harrison (1892–1965), a student of Becker and Whitehouse, who offers surprisingly brisk renditions of the Sarabandes from Suites Nos. 4 and 6, with Sir George Henschel (1850–1934) performing his own piano accompaniment.[101] This nineteenth-century style of playing – and especially the practice of playing the Cello Suites with piano accompaniment – would be supplanted completely by Casals's revolutionary, modern approach in his Bach recordings produced just over a decade later.

The Next Solo-Cello Editions: 1866–1900

Notes

1. Martin Barré, "La Fabrique du canon: Les Suites pour violoncelle de Bach avant Pablo Casals" (*mémoire en esthétique* document, Conservatoire national supérieur de musique et de danse de Paris, 2023), http://mediatheque.cnsmdp.fr, SyrtisID 39617013.
2. The early performance history of Bach's Violin Solos is surveyed in the following three studies: Zay David Sevier, "Bach's Solo Violin Sonatas and Partitas: The First Century and a Half" (parts 1 and 2), *BACH* 12, no. 2 (April 1981): 11–19; 12, no. 3 (July 1981): 21–29. Elizabeth I. Field, "Performing Solo Bach: An Examination of the Evolution of Performance Traditions of Bach's Unaccompanied Violin Sonatas from 1802 to the Present" (DMA diss., Cornell University, 1999). Dorottya Fabian, "Towards a Performance History of Bach's Sonatas and Partitas for Solo Violin: Preliminary Investigations," in *Essays in Honor of László Somfai on His 70th Birthday: Studies in the Sources and the Interpretation of Music*, ed. László Vikárius and Vera Lampert (Lanham, MD: Scarecrow Press, 2005), 87–108.
3. On historical cellists mentioned in this chapter, see Margaret Campbell, "Nineteenth-Century Virtuosi," in *The Cambridge Companion to the Cello*, ed. Robin Stowell (Cambridge: Cambridge University Press, 1999), 61–72; and Campbell, "Masters of the Twentieth Century," in Stowell, *The Cambridge Companion to the Cello*, 73–91.
4. Talle, revised preface, xxviii. See also David, Mendel, and Wolff, *New Bach Reader*, 224–25.
5. Altnikol's manuscript, catalogued at the Berlin State Library as P218 (fascicle 2), can be viewed at www.bach-digital.de. See Schulenberg, *The Keyboard Music of J. S. Bach*, 356–59; and Talle, revised preface, xxvi n. 22.
6. On questions of authorship, see Max H. Y. Wong, "Arrangements as a Creative Tool towards the Performance of J. S. Bach's Six Sonatas and Partitas for Solo Violin, BWV 1001–1006" (PhD diss., Royal College of Music, 2023), 77–82.
7. Hans T. David and Arthur Mendel, eds., *The Bach Reader: A Life of Johann Sebastian Bach in Letters and Documents*, rev. ed. (New York: W. W. Norton, 1972), 447.
8. Hans-Joachim Schulze, ed., *Bach Dokumente*, vol. 3, *Dokumente zum Nachwirken Johann Sebastian Bachs, 1685–1750* (Leipzig: Bach-Archiv, 1972), no. 695.
9. Translated in David, Mendel, and Wolff, *New Bach Reader*, 447–48.
10. Johann Philipp Kirnberger, *Die Kunst des reinen Satzes in der Musik*, 2 vols. (Berlin and Königsberg, 1774–79), 1:176.

Transmission, Performance, and Reception: 1720–c. 1900

11. Johann Friedrich Reichardt, "Einige Anmerkungen zu Forkels Schrift: Ueber Joh. Sebast. Bach," *Berlinische Musikalische Zeitung* 2, no. 51 (1806): 202.
12. Johann Traeg, *Verzeichniß alter und neuer sowohl geschriebener als gestochener Musikalien* (Vienna, 1799), 104.
13. See item no. 178 in Johann Gottfried Schwanberger, *Verzeichniß der von dem herzogl. Braunschw. Lüneb. Kapellmeister Schwanberg hinterlassenen beträchtlichen Sammlung von Musikalien* [...] (Braunschweig, 1806), 21.
14. Gerber, *Historisch-Biographisches Lexikon der Tonkünstler*, 1:92.
15. Ernst Ludwig Gerber, *Neues Historisch-Biographisches Lexikon der Tonkünstler*, 4 vols. (Leipzig, 1812–14), 1:215.
16. Alexandre-Étienne Choron and François-Joseph-Marie Fayole, *Dictionnaire historique des musiciens*, 2 vols. (Paris, 1810–11), 1:38. John Sainsbury, ed., *A Dictionary of Musicians* [...], 2 vols. (London, 1824), 1:49. Sainsbury's dictionary is based partly on Gerber's lexicon and partly on Choron and Fayole's dictionary.
17. Sainsbury, *A Dictionary of Musicians*, 1:49.
18. Amédée Méreaux, "Tablettes du pianiste et du chanteur: Les Clavecinistes (de 1637 à 1790)," *Le Ménestrel* 30, no. 51 (November 22, 1863): 409.
19. Louis-Pierre Norblin, ed., *Six Sonates ou études pour le violoncelle composées par J. Sébastien Bach, œuvre posthume* (Paris: Janet et Cotelle, [1824]), 1.
20. Norblin, *Six Sonates ou études*, 1.
21. Talle, revised preface, xxix.
22. Lynda MacGregor, "Norblin (de la Gourdaine), Louis (Pierre Martin)," in *Grove Music Online*, ed. Deane Root (published January 20, 2001). See also D. Kern Holoman, *The Société des Concerts du Conservatoire, 1828–1967* (Berkeley: University of California Press, 2004), 61. Some sources give the date of Norblin's appointment as professor at the Conservatoire as 1826; see, for example, C. Liégois and E. Nogué, *Le Violoncelle: Son histoire, ses virtuoses* (Paris: Constallat & Cie, [1913]), 132–33.
23. The only known copy of Norblin's edition is cataloged S-Skma, Mazer saml. B:35 at the Music and Theater Library of Sweden.
24. Bernhard Romberg, *Violoncell Schule* (Berlin, [1840]), 129. A version of the same remarks appears in the French version of Romberg's treatise: *Méthode de violoncelle* (Paris, [1840]), 129.
25. L. F. R. Fayet and B. Dutertre, eds., "Musique instrumentale," *Journal générale d'annonce des œuvres de musique, gravures, lithographies, etc. publiés en France et à l'étranger* 1, no. 16 (April 22, 1825): 127.

26. Heinrich Albert Probst, ed., *Six Sonates ou études pour le violoncelle solo composées par J. Sébastien Bach, œuvre posthume* (Leipzig: H. A. Probst, [1825]).
27. Zoltán Szabó, "Problematic Sources, Problematic Transmission: An Outline of the Edition History of the Solo Cello Suites by J. S. Bach" (PhD diss., Sydney Conservatorium of Music, 2016), 51.
28. Talle, revised preface, xxix–xxx.
29. A comparison of the Allemande from Suite No. 4 in the Norblin and Dotzauer editions reveals the latter's penchant for smoother bowings. See discussion in George Kennaway, "Bach Solo Cello Suites: An Overview of Editions," CHASE, accessed January 1, 2024, http://mhm.hud.ac.uk/chase/article/bach-solo-cello-suites-an-overview-of-editions-george-kennaway (site discontinued).
30. George Kennaway, *Playing the Cello, 1780–1930* (New York: Routledge, 2016), 111.
31. J. J. F. Dotzauer, *Méthode de violoncelle* (Mayence, [1823]), 60.
32. Talle, revised preface, xxx and xxxv.
33. E. van der Straeten and Lynda MacGregor, "Dotzauer, (Justus Johann) Friedrich," in *Grove Music Online*, ed. Deane Root (published January 20, 2001). See also Adriana Venturini, "The Dresden School of Violoncello in the Nineteenth Century" (MA thesis, University of Central Florida, 2009), 33–40.
34. Kennaway, "An Overview of Editions."
35. Robin H. Legge, "Music for the Violoncello," *Musical Opinion and Music Trade Review* 16, no. 186 (March 1893): 353.
36. Franz Pazdírek, ed., *Universal-Handbuch der Musikliteratur aller Zeiten und Völker*, 16 vols. (Vienna: Pazdírek & Co., 1904–10), 2:25.
37. Anonymous, review of various editions of Bach's music, *The Musical World* 8 (1838): 262.
38. For an overview, see Bradley Knobel, "Bach Cello Suites with Piano Accompaniment and Nineteenth-Century Bach Discovery" (DMA diss., Florida State University, 2006).
39. Edgar Stillman Kelley, "The Unpublished Bach-Schumann Violoncello Suites," *Music: A Monthly Magazine* 3, no. 6 (April 1893): 614.
40. Kelley, "The Unpublished Bach-Schumann Violoncello Suites," 612.
41. Anonymous, review of Monday Popular Concert, *The Musical World* 46, no. 2 (January 11, 1868): 19. The erroneous reference to a courante in G must refer to another suite in a minor key (either No. 2 or No. 5).
42. Anonymous, review of Monday Popular Concert, 19.
43. Charles Maclean, "[Leipzig] Bach Festival Impressions," *The Musical Times* 45, no. 741 (November 1, 1904): 734–35. On the challenges of executing chords on bowed string instruments, see

Robin Stowell, *The Early Violin and Viola: A Practical Guide* (Cambridge: Cambridge University Press, 2001), 81–82.
44. Field, "Performing Solo Bach," 5.
45. Robert Schumann, arr., *Suite III C-dur für Violoncello Solo, BWV 1009 für Violoncello und Klavier*, by J. S. Bach, ed. Joachim Draheim (Wiesbaden: Breitkopf & Härtel, 1985). Friedrich Wilhelm Stade, arr., *Joh. Seb. Bachs Compositionen für Violoncello solo. Mit Begleitung des Pianoforte* (Leipzig: Gustav Heinze, [1864]). Carl G. P. Grädener, arr., *Sechs Sonaten für das Violoncell von Joh. Seb. Bach mit Klavierbegleitung*, 2 vols. (Hamburg, [1871]).
46. Quoted in Draheim's preface to Schumann, *Suite III*, 8. See also Meebae Lee, "Rewriting the Past, Composing the Future: Schumann and the Rediscovery of Bach" (PhD diss., CUNY Graduate Center, 2011), 205–9.
47. Quoted in Draheim's preface to Schumann, *Suite III*, 8.
48. Paul Blackman, *Christian Reimers: A Spirited Performer* (Campbelltown, NSW: Paul Blackman, 2017), 25.
49. On Cabisius and Pruckner's performance, see Knobel, "Bach Cello Suites with Piano Accompaniment," 50–52. On Reimers and Reimann's, see Blackman, *Christian Reimers*, 89–90. See also Szabó, "Problematic Sources, Problematic Transmission," 236–38.
50. Kelley, "The Unpublished Bach-Schumann Violoncello Suites." See also Knobel, "Bach Cello Suites with Piano Accompaniment," 49–52.
51. For a detailed description and appraisal of Stade's arrangement (in the 1864 edition and later revisions), see Knobel, "Bach Suites with Piano Accompaniment," 56–69.
52. For an overview of later viola editions, see Thomas Tatton, "Bach Violoncello Suites Arranged for Viola: Available Editions Annotated," *Journal of the American Viola Society* 27 (Summer 2011): 5–27.
53. Anonymous, review of Altenburg Singakademie concert, *Neue Zeitschrift für Musik* 63, no. 48 (November 22, 1867): 425.
54. Anonymous, review of Altenburg Singakademie concert, *Neue Zeitschrift für Musik* 64, no. 49 (November 27, 1868): 424.
55. Kelley, "The Unpublished Bach-Schumann Violoncello Suites," 614. Grädener, preface to *Sechs Sonaten für das Violoncell von Joh. Seb. Bach mit Klavierbegleitung*, 1.
56. On the similar gap between eighteenth- and nineteenth-century musical aesthetics in Schumann's accompaniments, see Joel Lester, "Reading and Misreading: Schumann's Accompaniments to Bach's Sonatas and Partitas for Solo Violin," *Current Musicology* 56 (1994): 24–53.

The Next Solo-Cello Editions: 1866–1900

57. Yourij von Arnold [Yuri Karlovich Arnold], "Correspondenz: Leipzig" (review of First Euterpe Concert), *Neue Zeitschrift für Musik* 60, no. 45 (November 4, 1864): 396.
58. Thaddeus Egg [Joseph Bennett], "Charles Hallé's Pianoforte Recitals," *The Musical World* 51, no. 23 (June 7, 1873): 374. I am grateful to George Kennaway for sharing this source with me. On the authorship of items attributed to "Thaddeus Egg," see Joseph Bennett, "'Thaddeus Egg' Identified!," *The Musical Times and Singing Class Circular* 41, no. 683 (January 1, 1900): 52.
59. William Whitehouse, *Recollections of a Violoncellist* (London: The Strad Office, 1930), 93. Piatti's arrangement of Suite No. 1 was posthumously published by Schott.
60. Whitehouse, *Recollections of a Violoncellist*, 93; emphasis original.
61. Anonymous, review of Saturday Popular Concert, *The Athenæm* 3399 (December 17, 1892): 864.
62. Anonymous ("R. S."), review of Sixth Euterpe Concert, *Musikalisches Wochenblatt* 1, no. 5 (January 28, 1870): 74. The "Air" in question is an arrangement of the popular movement from the Orchestral Suite No. 3 in D Major (BWV1068).
63. Ferdinand David, arr., *Sechs Suiten für die Violine solo von Joh. Seb. Bach: Als Vorstudien zu den grossen Violin-Sonaten dieses Meisters* [. . .] (Leipzig: Gustav Heinze, [1866]).
64. Anonymous, "Music from Abroad," *Dwight's Journal of Music* 24, no. 24 (February 18, 1865): 397.
65. Yourij von Arnold, "Correspondenz: Leipzig," *Neue Zeitschrift für Musik* 61, no. 2 (January 6, 1865): 11.
66. Anonymous ("V."), items received from Merseburger Verlag, *The Violin Times: A Monthly Journal for Professional and Amateur Violinists and Quartet Players* 3, no. 35 (September 15, 1896): 43.
67. Joachim Raff, arr., *Sechs Sonaten für Violoncell componirt von Joh. Seb. Bach. Für Pianoforte bearbeitet von Joachim Raff* (Leipzig and Winterthur: J. Reiter-Biedermann, [1870–71]). Raff had previously published a solo-piano version of eighteen movements drawn from the Violin Solos, c. 1869. See Wong, "Arrangements as a Creative Tool," 256–59.
68. Agnes Zimmermann, arr., *Bourrée in C by J. S. Bach* (London, [1868]); *Bourrée in E♭ by J. S. Bach* (London, [1868]); and *Gavotte in G by J. S. Bach* (London, [1868]). Sara Heinze, arr., *Bach-Album : Beliebte Stücke für Pianoforte Solo von Joh. Seb. Bach*, rev. ed. (Leipzig, [1878]). I examined a reprint edition published as *Bach-Album: A Collection of Twenty-One Favorite Pieces for Pianoforte by Johann Sebastian Bach* (New York, 1898).

69. Anonymous, "Musique de piano," *Le Ménestrel* 70, no. 44 (October 30, 1904): 345. The announcement was repeated in several other issues in the following months.
70. Anonymous, review of *Gavotte en ré de John [sic] Sebastian Bach, transcrite pour piano par D. Brocca*, The Musical World 48, no. 48 (November 26, 1870): 789.
71. Ernst Pauer, "The Pianoforte Teacher: A Collection of Articles Intended for Educational Purposes," *Monthly Musical Record* 22, no. 260 (August 1, 1892): 176.
72. Friedrich Grützmacher, ed., *Six Sonates ou suites pour violoncelle seul par J. Seb. Bach. Édition nouvelle, revue et arrangée pour être exécuté aux concerts par Fr. Grützmacher* (Leipzig: C. F. Peters, [1866]); and Grützmacher, ed., *Sechs Suiten (Sonaten) für Violoncello solo von Joh. Seb. Bach, Original-Ausgabe* (Leipzig: C. F. Peters, [1867]). See also Szabó, "Problematic Sources, Problematic Transmission," 212–13. Szabó gives the date of the "original" edition as "c. 1884–88." However, an Edition Peters catalog published in 1869 indicates that both of Grützmacher's editions had already appeared. C. F. Peters, "Beste und billigste Klassiker-Ausgabe," unpaginated insert included in *Schwäbischer Merkur* (Stuttgart), no. 284 (December 1, 1869).
73. Campbell, "Nineteenth-Century Virtuosi," 68.
74. A detailed analysis of Grützmacher's concert edition appears in Szabó, "Problematic Sources, Problematic Transmission," 202–16.
75. Szabó, "Problematic Sources, Problematic Transmission," 205–6.
76. Kate Bennett Wadsworth, "'Precisely Marked in the Tradition of the Composer': The Performing Editions of Friedrich Grützmacher" (PhD diss., University of Leeds, 2017). See also Venturini, "The Dresden School," 70–72.
77. Friedrich Grützmacher, letter to Max Abraham of C. F. Peters, dated Dresden, September 17, 1888. Translated in Dimitry Markevitch, *Cello Story*, trans. Florence W. Seder (Princeton: Summy-Birchard Music, 1984), 62–63; emphasis original. For context, see Wadsworth, "Precisely Marked," 15–51. For a facsimile of this letter, see Ludolf Lützen, *Die Violoncell-Transkriptionen Friedrich Grützmachers: Untersuchung zur Transkription in Sicht und Handhabung der 2. Hälfte des 19. Jahrhunderts* (Regensburg: Gustav Bosse, 1974), 225–28.
78. Alfred Dörffel, ed., *Johann Sebastian Bach's Kammermusik*, vol. 6, *Solowerke für Violine, Solowerke für Violoncello* (Leipzig: Breitkopf & Härtel, 1877 [1879]). The volume is dated 1877, but since Dörffel's foreword is dated 1879, some scholars give the latter year as the publication date. This edition is widely available today in a 1988 reprint by Dover Publications.

The Next Solo-Cello Editions: 1866–1900

79. Julius Klengel, ed., *J. S. Bach, Sechs Suiten für Violoncell* (Leipzig: Breitkopf & Härtel, [1900]). Hugo Becker, ed., *Sechs Suiten (Sonaten) für Violoncello solo von Joh. Seb. Bach* (Leipzig: C. F. Peters, [1890]).
80. Anonymous, "Metropolitan Examinations of the Royal Academy of Music," *The Musical Standard* 21, no. 903 (November 19, 1881): 323.
81. Whitehouse, *Recollections of a Cellist*, 92.
82. Arthur Pougin, "Les Concours du Conservatoire," *Le Ménestrel* 75, no. 29 (July 17, 1909): 228. Pougin erroneously states that the piece was a sarabande in *B minor*, but another report confirms it was the sarabande in *D minor* (from Suite No. 2): Louis Laloy ("L. L."), "Résultats des concours," *Bulletin français de la Société internaional de musique* 5, nos. 8–9 (July 15, 1909): 782.
83. See, for example, Holoman, *The Société des Concerts du Conservatoire*, 249. For evidence correcting Holoman's misinterpretation, see Anonymous, "Concerts et auditions musicales," *Revue et gazette musicale* 42, no. 6 (February 7, 1875): 46. See also Katharine Ellis, *Music Criticism in Nineteenth-Century France: La Revue et gazette musicale de Paris 1834–80* (Cambridge: Cambridge University Press, 1995), 72.
84. Anonymous, "Nouvelles diverses," *Le Ménestrel* 30, no. 51 (November 22, 1863): 410.
85. J. d'Ortigue, review of chamber music concert organized by Alfred Holmes, *Journal du débats politiques et littéraires*, January 26, 1866: no pagination. The review identifies Müller only by surname, but other Parisian reviews of this period specify "Guillaume," indicating Wilhelm rather than his cellist uncle, Theodor (1802–1875).
86. Anonymous, concert advertisement, *L'Industriel alsacien: Journal de l'industrie* 32, no. 100 (November 22, 1866): no pagination.
87. Anonymous, concert advertisement, *Écho des Pyrénées* 6, no. 864 (November 26, 1879): no pagination. Anonymous, concert advertisement, *Écho des Pyrénées* 8, no. 1046 (January 19, 1881): no pagination.
88. Anonymous ("M."), concert review, *La Réforme* 14, no. 261 (September 18, 1897): no pagination.
89. Émile Mendel, "Nouvelles des théâtres," *Paris-Journal* 6, no. 30 (January 31, 1873): 3. See also Katharine Ellis, *Interpreting the Musical Past: Early Music in Nineteenth-Century France* (Oxford: Oxford University Press, 2008), 92.
90. Anonymous, "Société J.-S. Bach," *La revue musicale* 5, no. 20 (November 1, 1905): 528. On a broader Parisian trend away from "potpourri" concerts and toward more "serious" programming of complete works, see Ellis, *Interpreting the Musical Past*, 91–93.

Transmission, Performance, and Reception: 1720–c. 1900

91. Rudolph Viole, "Aus Berlin," *Neue Zeitschrift für Musik* 48, no. 14 (April 2, 1858): 151.
92. Anonymous ("S. R."), "Correspondenz: Dresden," *Neue Zeitschrift für Musik* 63, no. 20 (May 10, 1867): 178.
93. Otto Drönewolf, "Die Tonkünstler-Versammlung zu Meiningen," *Neue Zeitschrift für Musik* 63, no. 40 (September 27, 1867): 348.
94. Heinrich Schmidt ("Z"), "Correspondenz: Leipzig," *Neue Zeitschrift für Musik* 61, no. 7 (February 10, 1865): 56.
95. Hugo Wolf, *The Music Criticism of Hugo Wolf*, trans. and ed. Henry Pleasants (New York: Holmes & Meier, 1978), 234.
96. Hugo Becker and Dago Rynar, *Mechanik und Ästhetik des Violoncellspiels* (Vienna and Leipzig: Universal Edition, 1929), 201. Translation from Kennaway, *Playing the Cello*, 141.
97. Kennaway, *Playing the Cello*, 149–53.
98. Richard Taruskin, "Six Times Six: A Bach Suite Selection," in *The Danger of Music and Other Anti-Utopian Essays* (Berkeley: University of California Press, 2009), 66.
99. Klengel's c. 1927 recording with pianist E. Steinberger is included in Keith Harvey, ed., *The Recorded Cello: The History of the Cello on Record*, vol. 2 (Pearl, GEMM9984–86, 1992); and *Julius Klengel: A Celebration* (Cello Classics, CC1024, 2012), originally released 1936 by Decca-Polydor (DE7062).
100. Anonymous ("A. R."), review of Julius Klengel and E. Steinberger, Sarabande in D Major (Bach) and Adagio cantabile in G Major (Tartini), *The Gramophone* 14, no. 159 (August 1936): 112.
101. The Sarabandes from Suites Nos. 4 and 6 were originally released by His Master's Voice (respectively HMVD474 and HMVE205). The former is also included in *The Recorded Cello*, vol. 2. Prior to the accompanied recordings of the sarabandes, Harrison had previously made a solo recording of the Gigue from Suite No. 3 in 1918 (HMVD346). On Harrison's biography, see Hannah E. Collins, "International Influence on the Development of Cello Playing in England, 1870–1930: Robert Hausmann, August Van Biene, and Guilhermina Suggia" (DMA diss., CUNY Graduate Center, 2020), 197–200.

5
TRANSMISSION, PERFORMANCE, AND RECEPTION: AFTER C. 1900

Pablo Casals, the Modernist

It would be impossible to overstate Casals's transformative impact on the way Bach's Cello Suites are played in concerts and more broadly on the space they occupy in the cultural imagination (see Figure 5.1). Revered for his exuberant and soulful musicianship, Casals was responsible for establishing new performance norms for the Cello Suites that remain essentially compulsory today. Among these are the practice of playing a suite in its entirety (all six movements in order), with all repeats, and never with piano accompaniment. Casals did record the Andante from the Solo Violin Sonata No. 2 in A Minor (BWV 1003) with pianist Blas Net (1887–1948), in an arrangement by Alexander Siloti (1863–1945),[1] but he never recorded any movement from the Cello Suites with accompaniment.

Casals's interpretations of certain specific movements have also been broadly influential. Whereas nineteenth-century editions of the Prelude to Suite No. 2 indicate a moderately fast tempo, Casals's recording adopts a much slower tempo and a ruminating character. While the metronome marking is indicated as $\quarternote = 88$ in Hausmann's edition and as $\quarternote = 69$–72 in Becker's, Casals's recording is considerably slower, around $\quarternote = 48$–52, offering an interpretation that has (directly or indirectly) colored many cellists' performances. Casals was the first of many cello soloists to record the complete cycle of all six Cello Suites. Indeed, he was the first to make multiple recordings of the same movements, representing interpretations from different career stages – setting the model for some twenty cellists who have recorded two or more complete cycles.[2] Casals's best-known recordings of the complete Cello Suites date from 1936–39. He had previously made studio recordings of three individual movements of Suite No. 3 in 1915–16. In

Figure 5.1 Pablo Casals. Photo by Yousuf Karsh © 1954, reproduced by permission.

the early 1950s, when he was nearly seventy-five, he contemplated but ultimately did not complete a second studio cycle. However, a handful of live recordings survive from that late period.

Through Casals's influence, cellists today regard Bach's Cello Suites, more than any other repertoire, as music to explore and grapple with, day in and day out, from one's student years well into old age. Casals's long-standing morning routine – over some eight decades – began with playing music from the *Well-Tempered Clavier* (on piano) followed by the Cello Suites. According to an oft-recounted anecdote, when the octogenarian Casals was asked why he continued to practice Bach daily, long after he ceased giving concert tours, he would often quip, "I believe I am making progress."[3]

Beyond the concert hall and recording studio, cellists who have used Bach's Cello Suites to advocate for peace and an end to human suffering have followed a model established by Casals, whose fierce opposition to and self-imposed exile from Francoist Spain (and from all countries that recognized Franco's government) significantly disrupted his concert career and established him as a humanitarian figure. Other cellists who have used solo Bach in the same spirit include Mstislav Rostropovich (1927–2007), whose impromptu performance at Checkpoint Charlie, days after the Berlin Wall fell in 1989 (shown in Figure 5.2), is now commemorated with a statue.[4] A Bach performance by Yo-Yo Ma (b. 1955) at a US–Mexico border crossing in 2019 is the subject of a children's book.[5] A few years later, during the COVID-19 pandemic, Ma performed Bach for healthcare workers as part of his "Songs of Comfort" initiative, and in 2022 he performed outside the Russian embassy in Washington, DC, to protest that country's invasion of Ukraine. That same year, a haunting viral video of Suite No. 5 performed by Denys Karachevtsev (b. 1992) in the heavily bombarded streets of his hometown of Kharkiv, Ukraine, was used as a fundraiser for humanitarian aid.

Nevertheless, the received portrait of Casals as the "discoverer" of Bach's Cello Suites warrants correction.[6] In the minds of many musicians today, the performance history of the Cello Suites *begins* with Casals, who has come to be seen as a sui generis musician, an oracular or messianic figure who singlehandedly revived a long-lost repertoire. Writings about Casals regularly invoke Christian metaphors, casting the cellist as an evangelist (for reviving, interpreting, and spreading Bach's Cello Suites), as a martyr (for sacrificing his concert career for his antifascist principles), or as a sage sought out by pilgrims (for receiving musicians who traveled great distances to his remote home in Prades, France, to take lessons with him, often over an extended period). The romanticized image of Casals remains so broadly influential as to obscure the cellist as an actual historical figure.[7]

The notion of Casals as discoverer of the Cello Suites stems from a public persona that people around Casals – and to some extent the cellist himself – actively cultivated. The following foundational myth recounts the origin of Casals's lifelong relationship with the Cello Suites:

One day I told my father I needed especially to find some new solo music for the Café Pajarera. ... [W]e stopped at an old music shop near the harbor. I began browsing through a bundle of musical scores. Suddenly I came upon a sheaf of

Figure 5.2 Cellist Mstislav Rostropovich plays Bach at Checkpoint Charlie (Berlin), November 11, 1989. Reproduced by permission of Action Press.

Pablo Casals, the Modernist

pages, crumbled and discolored with age. They were unaccompanied suites by Johann Sebastian Bach – for the cello only! I looked at them with wonder: *Six Suites for Violoncello Solo*. What magic and mystery, I thought, were hidden in those words? I had never heard of the existence of the suites; nobody – not even my teachers – had ever mentioned them to me. I forgot our reason for being at the shop. All I could do was stare at the pages and caress them. That scene has never grown dim. Even today, when I look at the cover of that music, I am back again in the old musty shop with its faint smell of the sea. I hurried home, clutching the suites as if they were the crown jewels, and once in my room I pored over them. I read and reread them. I was thirteen at the time, but for the following eighty years the wonder of my discovery has continued to grow on me. Those suites opened up a whole new world. I began playing them with indescribable excitement. They became my most cherished music. I studied and worked at them every day for the next twelve years. Yes, twelve years would elapse and I would be twenty-five before I had the courage to play one of the suites in public at a concert. Up until then, no violinist or cellist had ever played one of the Bach suites in its entirety. They would play just a single section – a Saraband, a Gavotte or a Minuet. But I played them as a whole: from the Prelude through the five dance movements, with all the repeats that give the wonderful entity and pacing and structure of every movement, the full architecture and artistry. They had been considered academic works, mechanical, without warmth. Imagine that! How could anyone think of them as being cold, when a whole radiance of space and poetry pours forth from them! They are the very essence of Bach, and Bach is the essence of music.[8]

Since Bach's non-keyboard music was little known in Barcelona or Madrid during Casals's youth, he appears to have been unaware that the Cello Suites had been performed with some frequency in Paris, London, and especially throughout Germany by the time he first learned of their existence. His discovery narrative therefore overstates the obscure status of the Cello Suites, symbolized in his account by the decrepit condition of the score – a copy of Grützmacher's highly corrupt concert edition.[9] In emphasizing his teachers' ignorance of the Cello Suites and the dozen years that he devoted to studying them before performing publicly, Casals underscored his complete independence from any prior performances, interpretive traditions, or other influences.

By the 1910s and '20s, Casals frequently programmed Bach suites in his extensive international tours (often comprising 150–200 concerts per year), and his recordings of the complete cycle made in the late 1930s cemented their place in the concert repertoire. Casals understood his performance approach as a total break from his German precursors. Maurice Eisenberg (1900–1972), who had studied with Klengel and Becker before becoming a devoted student and friend of Casals, wrote that his earlier pair of teachers "still played the Bach suites like the most uninteresting Czerny exercises" and that "Casals brought the glimmer of light to the real Bach. ... Where all had been pomposity, he brought simplicity; where there had been deadness and pallor, he brought the breath of life and quickening of beauty and color."[10] Casals himself expressed much the same idea but in more explicitly nationalist terms, frequently contrasting his musical approach to Bach with the cold playing of "the German purists," remarking that "it was necessary to show the Germans how mistaken they were in their interpretation of their illustrious compatriot."[11] Klengel, for his part, also noted the irony "that it had taken a Spaniard to reveal Bach to his homeland."[12] According to Bernard Meillat, musical adviser of the Pau Casals Foundation, Casals's remarks about "German purists" stemmed from the mixed reception his performances received from some German critics.[13] Anti-German remarks dating from the 1950s presumably also reflected the broader historical and political context immediately after World War II.

Casals's rejection of his antecedents extended to all existing editions of the Cello Suites (mostly edited by Germans). By his own account, he played from a facsimile of Anna Magdalena Bach's manuscript and declined offers to produce his own edition, explaining that "my way of performing a work does not last longer than the actual playing of it."[14] Casals's own solo Bach recordings bear this assertion out. Many tracks contain minor variants – such as occasional chords or other details added or subtracted – that reflect his habit of practicing from memory and suggest a somewhat flexible conception of the musical text (see Example 5.1).[15] Such minor textual variants in Casals's concert performances and broadcasts attracted the attention of the Dutch music collector and bibliographer Anthony van Hoboken (1887–1983), an uncommonly meticulous listener.[16]

Where multiple recordings exist, Casals plays with different articulation and character. Whereas his studio recording of the

Pablo Casals, the Modernist

Example 5.1 Minor variants, as recorded by Pablo Casals.
a. Suite No. 1 in G Major, Gigue.
b. Suite No. 2 in D Minor, Allemande.
c. Suite No. 3 in C Major, Bourrée I.

Prelude to Suite No. 1 uses a legato bowing (slurring groups of eight notes), a live recording from 1955 uses three-note slurs followed by six separate bows.[17] No fewer than five Cello Suites editions have been published that claim to reflect Casals's interpretation(s), all of which contradict one another and depart from his recorded performances.[18]

Example 5.2 Suite No. 2 in D Minor, Prelude, as edited by Diran Alexanian. Reproduced by permission of Riemenschneider Bach Institute, Baldwin Wallace University.

Bernard Greenhouse (1916–2011), founding cellist of the Beaux Arts Trio, recounted the following instructive anecdote about studying Suite No. 2 with Casals over a three-week period:

> He insisted on certain bowings and fingerings that I had to write into my part exactly what he did. We went through the entire suite in this manner. . . . He then played the entire D minor Suite, changing all the bowings and fingerings from what he had taught me during the last three weeks. I sat there absolutely aghast as he finished. He smiled and said, "Now that's the real lesson of how to play Bach. You must learn it so well that you remember every single idea that you have had in your practice. Then you forget everything and improvise."[19]

Despite Casals's refusal to fix his interpretation on the written page, he apparently endorsed a highly unusual, innovative publication created by his close associate Diran Alexanian (1881–1954).[20] Hardly a performing edition at all, Alexanian's version represents a unique experiment as to what a modern Cello Suites edition could be. It was the first edition to include a facsimile of Anna Magdalena Bach's manuscript, followed by an idiosyncratic score showing a detailed voice-leading analysis (with upward and downward note stems indicating connections among implied polyphonic voices), plus fingerings and bowings intended to articulate the musical ideas suggested by the analysis (see Example 5.2).

Igor Stravinsky (1882–1971) once chided Casals for "playing Bach in the style of Brahms."[21] Although Casals is often described as a "Romantic" musician – a view that reflects his reputation as a solitary genius – in other respects he would better be characterized as a modernizer reflecting twentieth-century aesthetics. Casals was explicit about his contributions to progress and modernization in cello performance: "Of course, the study of 'cello-playing cannot stop at the stage to which I have brought it. . . . Much better than any treatises or editions, my pupils, all those who have had direct context with me, will carry on my method and my conceptions. They will transmit and develop them."[22] Largely self-taught and having rejected past traditions in cello performance, Casals cultivated a novel, forward-looking approach to playing Bach. Compared to the 1920s-era recordings by Harrison and Klengel, Casals's complete set of recordings from just over a decade later are notable for their wider vibrato, highly selective use of *portamento*, "spoken" (as opposed to "singing") performance style in many movements, and especially the spirited, often rough approach to bowing, notably on bass notes and final chords. Where Klengel's c. 1927 recording uses *portamento* on nearly every melodic skip or leap (either up or down), Casals's slides appear only at special moments and are almost exclusively ascending. A prominent example is in the Gigue from Suite No. 5, m. 61: In an otherwise rhythmically driving movement, Casals's wistful *portamento* marks a sudden shift to longer note values.

Taruskin underscores Casals's "deliberately scratchy, ugly, effortful tone" in his 1930s Bach recordings, as compared to his more refined sound in his near-contemporaneous recordings of nineteenth-century virtuoso cello music.[23] Kennaway hears affinities between Casals's Bach performances and modernist art and design, suggesting analogies to the expressive lines of cubism, the geometric structures of Bauhaus architecture, and the stripping away of ornament in the modern décor of Le Corbusier.[24] Two modernist cello techniques characteristic of Casals are a percussive style of fingering, sometimes bordering on left-hand pizzicato, and the rendering of certain *bariolage* figures as nearly simultaneous double stops, especially in fast tempos and loud dynamics (see Example 5.3). The quasi-pizzicato fingering style is clearly audible throughout Casals's recordings of the Sarabande

Example 5.3 *Bariolage* figures performed as double stops by Pablo Casals.
 a. Suite No. 2 in D Minor, Courante.
 b. Suite No. 3 in C Major, Gigue.

from Suite No. 5 (both the 1939 studio recording and the 1956 live recording).

Casals's influence has touched nearly all subsequent performers of the Cello Suites, but two extraordinary women with personal connections to Casals warrant special mention. One of the first women cellists with an international profile, the Portuguese Guilhermina Suggia (1888–1950) studied with Klengel in Germany and made successful debuts in London and Leipzig before moving to Paris to pursue a personal and professional relationship with Casals (1906–12). During this period, she was often billed on programs as "Mme P. Casals-Suggia," although the two were never married.[25] She eventually broke ties with Casals to settle in England.

Through Casals's influence, Suggia became interested in the Cello Suites and performed them often to critical acclaim. A London critic praised a solo performance, writing that in Suggia's hands "the Bach C major suite was an apotheosis."[26] Another couched his positive review in sexist, exoticizing language,

Figure 5.3 Augustus John, *Madame Suggia* (1920–23). Oil on canvas.
Reproduced by permission of Tate Images and the Estate of Augustus John.

describing Suggia as a "prima ballerina" and a "wondrous creature" whose solo Bach performance was suffused with "Andalusian witchery."[27] Among Suggia's few recordings was the complete Suite No. 3 (recorded 1924–27), which is regrettably not available in a modern release.[28] By Suggia's own account, she was playing the Cello Suites throughout the sittings for her well-known portrait by Augustus John (1878–1961), which depicts the cellist in a garnet-colored gown, posed in extreme profile, playing as if transported (see Figure 5.3).[29]

Figure 5.4 Lillian Fuchs. Photo by James Abresch (c. 1950). Reproduced by permission of the Juilliard Archives and Amédée Williams.

If Casals established the Cello Suites' special position in his instrument's repertoire, Lillian Fuchs (1901–95) did the same for the viola (see Figure 5.4). In 1947, when viola recital performances remained something of a novelty, she performed Suite No. 2 in a New York concert organized by The Musicians' Guild to critical and audience acclaim. That performance attracted the interest of a representative from the Decca label, who proposed that Fuchs record the complete cycle. Accepting the challenge, Fuchs devoted five years to a meticulous, systematic study of the Cello Suites, performing them at the Musicians' Guild on various occasions as preparation for her recording sessions.[30] Originally released in 1951–53, her Bach albums were out of print for half a century until they were finally reissued in 2005.[31]

Pablo Casals, the Modernist

Both her concerts and recording garnered rave reviews, even from critics who expressed doubts about the viola as a solo instrument:

> Lillian Fuchs, who is not much bigger than the viola she plays, appeared alone on the stage to play Bach's Suite in C minor. The viola is not an easy instrument to manipulate, and it takes craftsmanship to keep it interesting when it is unaccompanied. Miss Fuchs was equal to the occasion. She played with dignity, a well sustained tone and a grasp of Bach's music.[32]

A particularly impressive achievement is her performance of Suite No. 6, performed mostly in the original key of D major, stretching at times into the upper reaches of the viola's register. Fuchs's recording loosely follows an edition by her teacher, Kneisel Quartet violist Louis Svećenski (1862–1926), who made various adjustments to Suite No. 6 to render it more playable on viola, including transposing the Sarabande to G major.[33] Today, most violists transpose the entire Suite No. 6 to G major to place the piece in a more manageable register. The Scottish viola virtuoso William Primrose (1904–82) rejected that option but also considered the piece to be impractical in the original key, leading him to release a viola edition comprising only Suites Nos. 1–5.[34]

Fuchs's recording naturally invited comparisons to Casals's, as in the following glowing review: "Unaccompanied string playing capable of holding the attention of the listener is a rare commodity. Miss Fuchs, one of the greatest living violists, achieves this. ... One need not go back ... even to Casals for satisfaction in the two Suites, which are equally effective on cello or viola. Miss Fuchs is quite good enough. Need anyone say more?"[35] According to an anecdote recounted frequently by Fuchs's students, Casals – initially dubious that the Cello Suites could be performed with integrity on another instrument – invited Fuchs to play one or more suites for him while she was performing at his festival in Prades. Reluctantly accepting his invitation, she opted to play the demanding Suite No. 6. After she finished, an extended silence ensued, until Casals finally rendered his verdict: "On the viola, it sounds ... better!!!!"[36]

Music Analysis and the Cello Suites

Around the same time the Cello Suites were gaining greater notoriety, they also began to receive attention from music analysts interested in issues of voice leading, especially those who either played cello or who took an interest in Casals's performances. The Austro-Swiss music theorist Ernst Kurth (1886–1946), best known for writings on psychological and dynamic aspects of musical experience, had studied both cello and piano and maintained a lifelong interest in Bach's Violin Solos and Cello Suites. For Kurth, these repertoires were less oriented toward concert performances than to "solitary music-making of amateurs who seek profound [musical] values." Kurth added: "Even if their recent, undeniably more frequent reappearance in concert halls should be warmly welcomed ... their actual place is not the large concerts; they are chamber music in the best, narrowest, and most precious sense, intimate, and what is more, solitary art."[37]

Kurth's massive 1917 study of "linear counterpoint" uses excerpts from the Cello Suites and Violin Solos to illustrate several key concepts. In contrast to the four- and eight-bar periodicity Kurth associated with classical themes, he described how Baroque themes are launched with a motivic statement possessing "initial energy" (*Anfangsenergie*), which is continued by an ascending "spinning forth" (*Fortspinnung*) that carries the musical energy forward toward a peak, followed by a counterbalancing descent. The resulting "dynamic unit" (*Bewegungszug*) represents an arch that traces a path of rising and falling musical tension. Kurth introduced this concept with the Courante from Suite No. 6 (see Example 5.4), where the main motive ("Thema," m. 1) drives toward a high point on the note b (m. 3), with a compensatory relaxation arriving at the cadence (m. 8).[38] Kurth discusses further examples of *Fortspinnung* including the Preludes from Suites Nos. 2 and 3, the Sarabande from Suite No. 5, and examples from the Violin Solos.[39]

The Cello Suites also figure prominently in Kurth's discussion of "polyphonic melody," which identifies linear connections among nonconsecutive notes that establish the individual voices hidden within a solo-violin or solo-cello texture. For example, in

Example 5.4 Suite No. 6 in D Major, Courante, as analyzed by Ernst Kurth.

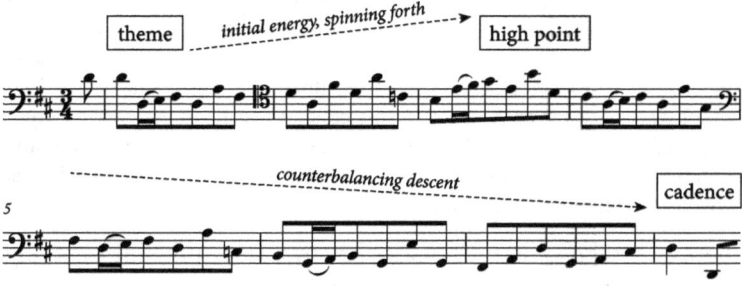

Example 5.5 Suite No. 2 in D Minor, Prelude (climax), as analyzed by Ernst Kurth.

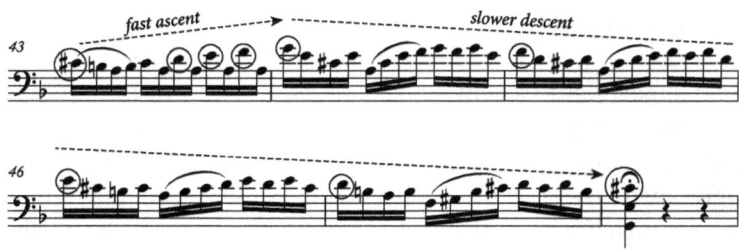

the Prelude to Suite No. 2 (shown in Example 5.5), Kurth traces a rising linear segment c♯′–d′–e′–f′–g′ (mm. 43–44), answered by a slower-moving descending line g′–f′–e′–d′–c♯′ (mm. 44–48, on the downbeats of each bar).[40]

The Viennese music analyst Heinrich Schenker (1868–1935) became interested in Bach's Cello Suites through hearing Casals's performances in both concerts and radio broadcasts. Usually sparing with praise, Schenker wrote the following effusive account of a 1926 concert in which Casals performed two concertos and Bach's Suite No. 3:

> An uncommonly strong instinct for synthesis, perhaps born from his incomparable understanding of the instrument! ... Casals senses a beauty in the construction of a greater unity; since at the same time he senses the technical means to express this beauty, he succeeds in fulfilling his feeling and he finds himself suddenly in possession of a new technique, which points him in the direction of new beauties – a circular flow of intellectual feeling and technique that, once

begun, continues forever. The understanding of synthesis is expressed unconsciously, primarily as a result of his plainly seeking points of clarity, reaching them easily, and leaving them just as easily so that he can proceed to new points of clarity. This makes his playing transparent, articulate; and even in polyphonic textures his instrument remains free of the thumping that is characteristic of others. It was not until an hour before the concert that I had the opportunity of seeing Be[c]ker's edition ... and I was afraid that Casals could, similarly, misinterpret Bach; I was all the more agreeably surprised to see that he had arrived as a synthesis by his own routes![41]

Schenker – whose diary includes several other praising accounts of Casals's performances of the Bach Cello Suites (with more mixed views of Casals in other repertoire) – suggested that Casals's performance somehow expressed an intuitive sense for the structure of musical "wholes" that Schenker was at that time attempting to theorize. Around the same time, Schenker began composing an essay about the Sarabande from the same suite, which appeared the following year.[42] At the heart of the essay is a Schenkerian "graph" showing analytical layers progressing from the most detailed – including almost all notes in Bach's score – to progressively simpler, more abstract versions, revealing a hidden C major melodic scale that Schenker regarded as expressing the Sarabande's fundamental line (*Urlinie*). Schenker closes his essay with suggestions for dynamic shadings that might express that line, ideas that he might well have heard in the Casals concert that he so loved.[43]

Gerrit Hulshoff (1895–1975) published the first known monograph (book-length study) of Bach's Cello Suites in the Netherlands in 1944.[44] Hulshoff had been introduced to the Cello Suites by his teacher, Charles van Isterdael (1873–1962), but he ultimately pursued a nonmusical career as a maritime engineer for the Surabaya Dry Dock Company (Droogdok Maatschappij Soerabaja), where he was based from 1921 to 1938. The scant information available about Hulshoff's cello playing suggests that he was an accomplished but amateur performer. A 1936 concert he played with the Surabayan Quartet earned an enthusiastic review.[45]

When he hosted the Budapest String Quartet in his Surabaya home, the quartet's cellist, Mischa Schneider (1904–85), discussed the inadequacy of all available editions of the Cello Suites with

Hulshoff, prompting the latter to devote ten years to studying and writing about textual, analytical, and interpretive issues in the Cello Suites. Addressed to a readership of cellists, Hulshoff's book is remarkably thorough and multifaceted, with detailed discussions of discrepancies among editions and manuscript sources, single-voice polyphony, performance nuances (articulation, dynamics, rubato, vibrato), instrumental issues relating to *scordatura* (Suite No. 5) and five-string cello (Suite No. 6), and finally a formal, motivic, and stylistic analysis of all six Cello Suites. Given the book's originality, scope, degree of detail, and extensive bibliography, Hulshoff's study could only have been written by a cellist who had studied and reflected on the Cello Suites over many years, considering in detail the performance problems raised by various editions – especially about slurs and chord rolling – and consulting manuscript sources for clarification.

Drawing on his deep knowledge of the suites, he offered the following concise characterizations of each one:

No. 1 simple, charming.
No. 2 full of internal conflict.
No. 3 brilliant, focused on outward contact.
No. 4 solemn, broad.
No. 5 somber, introspective.
No. 6 virtuosic, full of the joy of life.[46]

Gifted at explaining complex musical ideas in simple language, Hulshoff compared ideas of single-voice polyphony (adapted from Kurth and Alexanian) to the capacity of line drawings to suggest both dimensionality and shade.[47] Where Kurth's analyses are oriented toward the abstract and the psychological, Hulshoff's approach emphasizes concrete performance applications.

Particularly of interest are Hulshoff's remarks about Casals's recordings, which had only just appeared as Hulshoff was writing his book. Despite Hulshoff's fastidious attention to the musical text – motivating his detailed examination of discrepant notes and slurs – he nevertheless reveled in the free approach embraced by Casals. Hailing Casals as the "ingenious re-creator ... who has liberated the suites from the grip of partial oblivion and neglect," Hulshoff wrote: "Respect for Bach's music itself – more important than respect for the notes! – requires that one avoid anything dry and mathematically flattening. Countless solutions are possible. Whoever possesses imagination and can express it will forever discover new possibilities. One should never consider a particular solution to be final or beyond improvement."[48]

To the Present Day

To fully survey the performance and reception history of the Cello Suites from the postwar period to the present would fill an entire book. This final section traces various threads that reveal a trajectory toward greater innovation and experimentation in the performance of Bach's Cello Suites as well as a broader resonance in popular culture. These threads should be taken as representative rather than exhaustive. If the Cello Suites had remained somewhat obscure when Casals first began performing them in the early twentieth century, by a century later the Sarabande from Suite No. 1 (as recorded by an unknown cellist) was included as a preset ringtone for several models of Nokia mobile phones used by over 50 million people, evincing a worldwide reach but also a kind of commodification of Bach's music.[49]

The Cello Suites have continued to be performed and recorded widely by students, amateurs, and world-class artists, and they are commonly required in auditions and international competitions. Whereas concert reviewers had once questioned their suitability as concert repertoire, in 1995 a *New York Times* critic asserted as self-evident that the Cello Suites "are not only the greatest music written for the instrument but in the running for the greatest music ever written."[50] Numerous cellists have continued to publish performing editions, although in recent decades musicians have increasingly opted to use "clean" *Urtext* editions and to consult manuscript facsimiles – especially of Anna Magdalena Bach's copy (Source A) – to choose their own bowings and articulations. Almost without exception, recordings on cello now take the form of complete cycles. The Grammy Award for Best Instrumental Soloist Performance has twice been awarded to such albums: in 1984 to the first of Ma's three recordings and in 1998 to the fifth (!) and final recording of the cycle by János Starker (1924–2013).[51]

To the Present Day

A growing number of cellists have tackled the Herculean feat of performing all six Cello Suites, usually in a pair of concerts but sometimes in a single marathon event. The earliest known cellist to do so was Henri Honegger (1904–92), a Swiss-born student of Klengel, Casals, and Alexanian. Honegger played the complete cycle for the first time in 1946 in London's Cowdray Hall and, over the next decade, in Wigmore Hall, Royal Festival Hall, various Dutch venues including the Concertgebouw, and at the University of Michigan. A critic who attended the 1946 cycle expressed doubts about the Cello Suites cycle as a suitable concert program, preferring a recital program that included only one suite and describing Honegger as "conscientious ... [but lacking] the emotional instinct necessary to give sufficient color and contrast."[52] But a pair of 1949 recitals in which Honegger performed the Cello Suites cycle in The Hague's Pulchri Studio received a glowing review. That critic praised Honegger's "exceptional" technical talent, describing his interpretation as a "clear, compelling presentation of the composer's intentions," unlike that of other performers, who offered either "a Romanticized Bach" or a "quasi-spiritualized" and "sterile" one.[53] A similarly positive review of his 1955 Cello Suites cycle in Wigmore Hall remarks that his "outlook is so musicianly that his renditions always give genuine satisfaction."[54]

Max Oróbio de Castro (1887–1962), a student of Isaäc Mossel (1870–1923) and Casals, also gave critically acclaimed performances of the Cello Suites cycle in Amsterdam and The Hague in 1948–50, overlapping with Honegger's tours in the same cities and sometimes drawing comparisons. An anonymous critic praised his trilogy of Cello Suites concerts at the Diligentia Theater in The Hague (1948–49) as "an initiative that requires not only craftsmanship but also artistic courage."[55] Another generally positive review of the same concerts characterizes his Romantic style of phrasing as "representing more the emotional life of a nineteenth-century [composer] than that of Bach or his contemporaries."[56] A review of Oróbio de Castro's Concertgebouw recital featuring Suites Nos. 4–6 describes Suite No. 5 as a highlight, observing that Suite No. 6 "acquires ... something forced, something uncomfortable" when performed on a four-string cello, resulting in a different timbre than the composer had imagined.[57]

The ensuing decades saw several cellists playing the complete cycle in New York: David Freed (1910–98) in 1956, George Neikrug (1919–2019) in 1979, Norman Fischer (b. 1949) in 1984, Mischa Maisky (b. 1948) in 1987, and Rostropovich in 1987 for his sixtieth birthday.[58] The British-Israeli cellist Thelma Yellin (1895–1959) performed the cycle in a trio of 1950 broadcasts on Kol Yisrael, the Israeli public radio service,[59] and Uzi Wiesel (1927–2019) presented the suites in a pair of concerts at the Tel Aviv Museum in 1971. Besides these one-off special events, many cellists have performed this program more widely on concert tours. Carlos Prieto (b. 1937) marked the composer's tercentennial with recitals of the complete Cello Suites in New York, Paris, and throughout India, as well as performances of individual suites in Mexico and the USSR.[60]

Ma performed the cycle at a BBC Prom in the Royal Albert Hall in 2015 for a sold-out audience of over 5,000 people. He marked the release of his third Cello Suites album (2018) with *The Bach Project*, a sprawling tour on six continents, comprising thirty-six Bach concerts and "days of action" engaging extensively with local community organizations and artists (see Figure 5.5).[61] Another community-oriented project began informally when Dale Henderson (b. 1976) began regularly performing the Cello Suites in New York City subway stations in 2010. His efforts sparked a grassroots movement called Bach in the Subways that has included hundreds of free, public performances of Bach's music in some forty countries.[62]

The historical performance movement – whereby musicians experiment with period instruments and treatises to imagine how eighteenth-century musicians may have played – gained momentum particularly in the Low Countries starting around the 1950s and '60s. Initially a countercultural movement involving Baroque specialists only, it has come to have a more widespread influence, including on cellists who use modern instruments. If many modern cellists have traditionally aspired toward a post-Romantic aesthetic of long, sustained melodic lines, recently more players have adopted a Baroque-influenced approach including audible

Figure 5.5 Yo-Yo Ma with local drummers in Dakar (Senegal), part of his thirty-six-city tour for *The Bach Project*. Photo by Austin Mann © 2020, reproduced by permission. For a full color version of this figure, please visit www.cambridge.org/9781316511770 and navigate to the Resources tab.

separation between slurs and sometimes light ornamentation. This aesthetic has had a notable influence on the performance of chords. Whereas some older performance editions encourage cellists to "hide" chordal bass notes – playing them before the beat, as grace notes, to minimize disruption of the melodic line (as in Example 4.3) – many cellists today execute chords more similarly to harpsichord players, emphasizing bass notes on the beat and rolling chords at various speeds depending on the music's character. This approach relies on the resonance of the performance space and the imagination of the audience to hear continuities even when the melody is punctuated by bass notes or chords.

While cellists had long known that Suite No. 6 was originally composed for a five-string instrument, the historical performance's spirit of experimentation finally encouraged some Baroque cellists to try it on such instruments. This "revival" is nevertheless paradoxical since it is not certain whether any cellists ever actually played Suite No. 6 on a five-string instrument during Bach's lifetime. Before the historical performance movement, the only cellist known to have played on such an instrument is Henri Bosmans (1856–96), principal of the Concertgebouw Orchestra, who commissioned a five-string cello specifically to play Suite No. 6. An anonymous reviewer of Bosmans's 1893 performance of that suite predicted that five-string cellos would not become commonplace since the added E string is "little in keeping with the character of the cello" and resembles "a baritone singer who found a way to also reproduce high notes from the tenor register." Yet the reviewer praised Bosmans's excellent playing, adding that a lesser artist would not be able to sustain the audience's interest throughout a full suite for unaccompanied cello.[63]

A 1960 album by Annlies Schmidt-de Neveu (1915–2010) is the earliest known recording to adopt a period approach, including the use of a five-string instrument for Suite No. 6; it is also the earliest complete recording on cello by a woman.[64] Other early period recordings using five-string instruments for Suite No. 6 include a 1965 album by Nikolaus Harnoncourt (1929–2016) and a 1977 release by Bylsma.[65] The historical performance movement has also motivated experimentation with – or revival of? – performance on viola da spalla, notably by Sigiswald Kuijken (b. 1944) and Dmitry Badiarov (b. 1969).[66] More recently, period cellists have also begun reviving the viol-like underhand bow hold used by many seventeenth- and eighteenth-century players (see discussion in Chapter 1).

Beyond cellists and violists, other instrumentalists have increasingly "co-opted" the Cello Suites (or portions thereof) as repertoire for study, concert performance, and recording. Notable contributions on double bass include recordings by François Rabbath (b. 1931), Richard Hartshorne (b. 1943), and Edgar Meyer (b. 1960).[67] Hartshorne may be the first bassist to record all six suites and the only one thus far to perform all six in concert.[68] Albums featuring some or all of the Bach Cello Suites in transcriptions for various instruments have been released, including flute,[69] trombone,[70] marimba,[71] classical guitar,[72] viol (viola da gamba),[73] banjo,[74] and ukulele,[75] with a still wider range of instruments represented on informal recordings on YouTube. While student violinists have long studied excerpts from the Cello

To the Present Day

Suites, four recent recordings by professional violinists (using period and modern instruments) represent a new trend.[76]

Bach's Cello Suites inspired later composers to create new suites for solo cello. Many have entered the standard recital repertoire, including solo suites by Max Reger (1873–1916), Gaspar Cassadó (1897–1966), Ernest Bloch (1880–1959), Benjamin Britten (1913–76), and Hans Gál (1890–1987).[77] The finale of *Cello Concert* (1966) by Lukas Foss (1922–2009), titled "Sarabande by Bach," refracts the Sarabande from Suite No. 5 by having the cello soloist "compete" with a distorted, prerecorded "Rival Cello." *Cello Suite Variation* (2000) by Christian Wolff (b. 1934) is an abstract reimagining of three movements of Suite No. 1.

The album *Bach Recomposed* (2018) by cellist-composer Peter Gregson (b. 1987) represents a reworking of the Cello Suites with looped synth patterns and postminimalist techniques.[78] The album *Step into the Void* (2020) by Mike Block (b. 1982) includes the complete Cello Suites plus a companion album of live "companion tracks" with free-improvised music created with sound artist Barry Rothman.[79] *Preludes* (2022) by Julia MacLaine (b. 1982) alternates the six preludes with six corresponding "response" compositions commissioned from Canadian composers that represent a cross section of that country's multiculturalism, including music influenced by Indigeneity, Maritimes fiddle music, and Indian Carnatic music.[80] The *Fragments* project by Alisa Weilerstein (b. 1982) comprises six concert programs, each interweaving the movements of a single Cello Suite with commissioned solo-cello works by contemporary composers.[81]

Beyond "classical" music, the Prelude to Suite No. 1 has been covered, sampled, or used as a riff in a surprising variety of popular genres. Examples include Genesis guitarist Steve Hackett's instrumental "Horizons" (1972), Laurindo Almeida's bossa nova tune "Unaccustomed Bach" (1978), folk guitarist John Renbourn's loose transcription "Prelude in G" (2011), Sweetbox's Euro-pop song "Here Comes the Sun" (2006), I'm Not a Pilot's alt-rock cover of Radiohead's "Creep" (2012), The Piano Guys' eight-part multi-track pop cover "The Cello Song" (2012), NU'EST's J-pop song "Flying Angel" (2014), Derek Brown's jazz sax paraphrase "Cello

Suite, No. 1" (2016), Nora en Pure's house track "Enchantment" (2020), Fire & Grace's folk rendition of Suite No. 1 (2021), Sebastián Yatra and Myke Tower's Latin pop song "Pareja del Año" (2021), and 2Cellos' crossover instrumental songs "Halo" and "Sweet Child O' Mine" (2021).

Ma released an uncommonly ambitious, interdisciplinary project titled *Inspired by Bach* in 1997. The project comprised not only a standard album – Ma's second recorded cycle[82] – but also a series of six films, each suite in relation to another artform:

> Suite No. 1: *The Music Garden* (directed by Kevin McMahon), with landscape architect Julie Moir Messervy.
> Suite No. 2: *The Sound of the Carceri* (directed by François Girard), with etchings by eighteenth-century architect Giovanni Battista Piranesi.
> Suite No. 3: *Falling Down Stairs* (directed by Barbara Willis Sweete), with choreographer Mark Morris.
> Suite No. 4: *Sarabande* (directed by Atom Egoyan), with a dramatic movie featuring actors Arsinée Khanjian and Lori Singer.
> Suite No. 5: *Struggle for Hope* (directed by Niv Fichman), with Kabuki actor Bandō Tamasaburō.
> Suite No. 6: *Six Gestures* (directed by Patricia Rozema), with Olympic-champion ice dancers Jane Torvill and Christopher Dean.[83]

Each film has a distinct style and character: Where *Falling Down Stairs* is a traditional documentary following Morris grappling with his choreographic interpretation of Bach's musical gestures, *Sarabande* cleverly weaves together character studies of a fictional taxi driver, real estate agent, and doctor, each viewed through the prism of their relationships to Ma's music. The unifying thread across *Inspired by Bach* is Ma's charismatic presence and his vision of the Cello Suites as a timeless cultural heritage that transcends boundaries of artistic discipline, historical period, and culture.

The Cello Suites have inspired or been featured in many works of art, literature, and multimedia. Several visual artists have produced abstract works representing various movements or recordings, including Hildegard Haas's geometric watercolors (c. 1960s), Fiona Robinson's dynamic charcoal drawings (2013–15), and cellist Amy Kang's vibrant paintings that map Bach's notes

To the Present Day

and harmonies onto a colorful matrix (2013–18). Writings about the Cello Suites include novels,[84] short stories,[85] memoirs,[86] nonfiction,[87] and (unfortunately) conspiracy theory.[88] Science fiction writer Ursula K. Le Guin described her published sets of stories as "story suites," drawing an analogy specifically to Bach: "The several movements of a Bach cello suite don't assume a unified form like a sonata, and yet each of the six suites is undoubtedly an entity, unified by more than a common key."[89] Theater van de Heelheid's theatrical project *BACH/LUTHER Cellosuites* (2023) weaves together texts by Martin Luther and live performance of selected movements from the Cello Suites into a narrative about the composer's life, music, and faith.

Several works of ballet and modern dance have incorporated onstage cellists performing music from Bach's suites. The most prominent example is Jerome Robbins's *A Suite of Dances* (1994), created for Mikhail Baryshnikov and cellist Wendy Sutter (b. 1967) at the White Oak Dance Project. The original production was performed on an extensive world tour, and the piece continues to be performed in revivals (see Figure 5.6).[90] More recent dance creations incorporating onstage cellists include Heinz Spoerli's *Bach Cello Suites: In den Winden im Nichts* (*In the Winds of Nothingness*, 2003) for the Zurich Ballet; Helen Lai's *Plaza X* (2011) for the Hong Kong City Contemporary Dance Company (combining dance and figure skating); Jorma Elo's *Bach Cello Suites* for the Boston Ballet (2015); Anne Teresa De Keersmaeker's *Mitten Wir im Leben sind* (*In the Midst of Life*, 2017) created with cellist Jean-Guihen Queyras (b. 1967); and Sandra Brown's *Hope* (2020) for the Colorado Ballet. Other choreographers have used live performance of the Cello Suites on instruments besides cello, such as Antonio Ruz's *Double Bach* (2016) for the Compañia Antonio Ruz (with amplified bass played pizzicato) and Spoerli's untitled choreography (2016) for legendary ballerina Alessandra Ferri and Sting (playing classical guitar). Many champion figure skaters, including Olympic medalists Mao Asada and Evgeni Plushenko, have skated to Bach's Cello Suites in competitions or exhibitions.

Dozens of film soundtracks prominently feature the Cello Suites, either in the underscore or in diegetic performances. Examples range from the serious – Anand Tucker's *Hilary and*

Transmission, Performance, and Reception: After c. 1900

Figure 5.6 Dancer Eno Peçi and cellist Ditta Rohmann perform Jerome Robbins's *A Suite of Dances* (1994). Photo by Ashley Taylor © 2021. Reproduced by permission of the Robbins Rights Trust and the Vienna State Ballet. For a full color version of this figure, please visit www.cambridge.org/9781316511770 and navigate to the Resources tab.

Jackie (1998), Roman Polanski's *The Pianist* (2002), Peter Weir's *Master and Commander: The Far Side of the World* (2003), Pere Portabella's *Die stille vor Bach* (*The Silence before Bach*, 2007), and Yaron Zilberman's *A Late Quartet* (2014) – to the comedic – Gillies MacKinnon's *A Simple Twist of Fate* (1994) and Todd Phillips's *The Hangover II* (2011).[91] Tony Scott's horror film *The Hunger* (1983) centers on a pair of vampires, one of whom (played by David Bowie) is a cellist who performs the Prelude to Suite No. 1. Bach's cello sarabandes in particular figure in several films by Ingmar Bergman – *Journey into Autumn* (1954), *Through the Glass Darkly* (1961), *Cries and Whispers* (1972), *Autumn Sonata* (1978), and especially his eponymous final film, *Saraband* (2003).[92] Woody Allen, an admirer of Bergman, likewise incorporated cello sarabandes in *Another Woman* (1988) and *Small Time Crooks* (2000).[93] Stephen Sondheim's musical *A Little Night Music* (1973) – inspired by Bergman's *Smiles of a Summer Night* (1955) – features a solo-cello sarabande played by the character Henrik.

In an unlikely trend – or perhaps one calibrated for social media – several recent documentaries and promotional films follow cellists hiking through mountainous regions to perform the Cello Suites outdoors and at altitude. Mario Brunello (b. 1960) performed solo Bach atop Mount Fuji in 2007 and has made other videos in the Italian Alps and atop Mount Etna (Sicily) in 2019.[94] Dane Johansen (b. 1984) hiked the 600-mile Camino de Santiago (Spain), recording the Cello Suites' thirty-six movements in as many churches along the way.[95] Under the auspices of the No Borders festival, 2Cellos founding member Luka Šulić (b. 1987) filmed a performance on the highest peak of the snowy Kanin Mountains.[96] The short documentary *Andante* follows Ruth Boden (b. 1977) on a journey through the Wallowa Mountains (Oregon) as she climbs to play Bach at a 3,000-meter summit.[97] If performing Bach's Cello Suites represents a journey or a challenge for any cellist to accomplish, these films depict that metaphor concretely.[98]

Turning now to television: Hwang Ui Kyung's K-drama *Naeil's Cantabile* (also known as *Tomorrow's Cantabile*, 2014) follows the personal and professional tribulations of a coterie of fictional music students. In a pivotal scene in episode 7, the suave and gifted cellist Lee Yoon Hoo performs the Prelude to Suite No. 1, revealing the depth of his artistry but also signs of a degenerative illness that eventually will lead him to give up the cello for conducting. Gregson's "recomposed" version of the Cello Suites was used in soundtracks throughout the first season of Paolo Sorrentino's *The New Pope* (2020) and in an emotionally intense ballroom scene from the season one finale of Shonda Rhimes's *Bridgerton* (2020). The episode "Girls Are Angry Too" from the third season of Nick Kroll's *Big Mouth* (2019) opens to comedic effect with Maury the Hormone Monster reciting a poem he wrote that juxtaposes an elevated literary tone with adolescent sex jokes, accompanied by solo-cello music modeled after the Prelude to Suite No. 1. Katharina Eyssen's series *Die Kaiserin* (*The Empress*) includes a scene in the season 1 (2022) episode "The Hunt" depicting newlywed Empress Elisabeth of Austria taking tea in a garden with her ladies-in-waiting, as a string-quartet arrangement of the Bourrée I from Suite No. 3 sounds in the underscore. In a dramatic montage from the series premiere of Tim Burton's *Wednesday* (2022), protagonist Wednesday Addams plays a cello solo from sheet music showing the Prelude to Suite No. 1, with handservant Thing turning pages (although the music actually played and heard is a cello cover of "Paint It Black" by the Rolling Stones).

In Fujisaku Jun'ichi's anime series *Blood+* (2005–6), the mysterious, cello-playing chevalier Hagi plays Suite No. 5 in various episodes, sometimes triggering vague flashbacks in his love interest, protagonist Otonashi Saya. Two anime series have incorporated the Prelude to Suite No. 1: Takemoto Yashuhiro's *Hyouka* (2012) uses it (nondiegetically) in several episodes. In the episode "Lies and Silence" from Anno Hideaki's series *Neon Genesis Evangelion* (1995), the teenage protagonist Ikari Shinji plays the Prelude to Suite No. 1 on his cello to express nostalgia for the pre-apocalyptic world and to convey emotions that are otherwise difficult for him to communicate.[99] Perhaps since this prelude's abstraction allows it to be adapted for many contexts, it has been used in a variety of American television commercials – for such motley brands as American Express, Cadillac, La-Z-Boy, and Papa Murphy's pizza[100] – as well as in some 250,000 TikTok videos on most every topic imaginable.

This survey ends around spring 2020, during the "lockdown" phase of the COVID-19 pandemic. At that time, many musicians found themselves isolated in their homes with all upcoming concerts canceled. These challenging circumstances led many string players to turn to the Violin Solos and Cello Suites. As I began to compose this book, my social media feeds were filled with dozens of musicians sharing homemade videos of unaccompanied Bach on a daily basis. Some musicians were inspired to turn the dire circumstances into a challenge for ambitious recording projects. Weilerstein's #36DaysofBach project involved recording one movement each day for thirty-six days, with regular Facebook Live chats to discuss the music with fans. Her recordings were subsequently released as an album.[101] Weilerstein's project in turn inspired bassist Nina DeCesare (b. 1992) to undertake a similar project under the same hashtag (but without a culminating album), an impressive undertaking given the imposing challenges several movements pose on the bass.

Why solo Bach during a global pandemic? This music is suitable for recording at home, and its many short movements are convenient to share over streaming or social media platforms. In the minds of some musicians and listeners, even Bach's secular music may evoke a sense of "the spiritual" that offered comfort during an uncertain time. Finally, for musicians who have lived with the Violin Solos and Cello Suites from childhood through adulthood, this repertoire offers technical and musical challenges that are enriching to explore, again and again, throughout a lifetime.

Notes

1. Pablo Casals, *Encores and Transcriptions*, vol. 2, *1927–30* (Naxos, 8.110976, 2004); originally released in 1929 by His Master's Voice (DB1404).
2. On Casals's initial reluctance to record the Cello Suites, see Oskar Falta, "A Great Wave in the Evolution of the Modern Cellist: Diran Alexanian and Maurice Eisenberg, Two Master Cello Pedagogues from the Legacy of Pablo Casals" (DMA diss., University of British Columbia, 2019), 21–22.
3. See Robert Snyder's documentary *Pablo Casals* (New York: Mannes College of Music, 1955), 8:47.
4. Brian Wise, "Why Are Cellists So Often Involved in Political Causes?," *Strings Magazine* 37, no. 315 (November–December 2023): 40–44.
5. Joanna Ho and Teresa Martinez, *Playing at the Border: A Story of Yo-Yo Ma* (Fairfax: Literary Ideas, 2021).
6. Martin Barré, "Casals, Discoverer of Bach's Cello Suites?" (paper presented at "Casals 50: Romantique ou moderne?," Maison Heinrich Heine, Paris, November 16, 2023).
7. See, for example, Anna Benson Gyles's documentary *Pau Casals* (London: BBC TV, 1991) and Eric Siblin's book *The Cello Suites: J. S. Bach, Pablo Casals, and the Search for a Baroque Masterpiece* (New York: Atlantic Monthly Press, 2009).

8. Pablo Casals, *Joys and Sorrows: Reflections by Pablo Casals as Told to Albert E. Kahn* (London: MacDonald and Co., 1970), 46–47.
9. The score is preserved today at the Pau Casals Archive at the National Archive of Catalonia. It is briefly visible in Gyles's documentary *Pau Casals*, around the thirty-minute mark.
10. Maurice Eisenberg, "Casals and the Bach Suites," *The New York Times* (October 10, 1943): X7. On Eisenberg's relationship to Casals, see Falta, "A Great Wave," 15–22.
11. J. Ma. Corredor, *Conversations with Casals*, trans. André Mangeot (New York: E. P. Button & Co., 1957), 98, translation lightly emended. For Casals's views about German "purism," see p. 62 and throughout. See also John H. Planer, "Sentimentality in the Performance of Absolute Music: Pablo Casals's Performance of Saraband from Johann Sebastian Bach's Suite No. 2 in D Minor for Unaccompanied Cello, S. 1008," *The Musical Quarterly* 73, no. 2 (1989): 230.
12. H. L. Kirk, *Pablo Casals: A Biography* (New York: Holt, Rinehart, and Winston, 1974), 216.
13. Personal communication, email dated February 6, 2024.
14. Corredor, *Conversations with Casals*, 210.
15. Rudolf von Tobel, *Pablo Casals*, 2nd ed. (Zurich: Rotapfel-Verlag, 1945), 76.
16. Heinrich Schenker, diary entry dated March 23, 1926, transcr. Marko Deislinger, trans. William Drabkin, http://schenkerdocumentsonline.org/documents/diaries/OJ-03-08_1926-03/r0023.html.
17. The live 1955 recording is featured in Snyder's documentary *Pablo Casals*, 9:40.
18. Szabó, "Problematic Sources, Problematic Transmission," 183.
19. Tim Janof, "Conversation with Bernard Greenhouse (November, 1998)," Cello Bello, accessed January 1, 2024, www.cellobello.org/cello-blog/internet-cello-society-archive/conversation-with-bernard-greenhouse.
20. Diran Alexanian, ed., *J. S. Bach, Six Suites pour violoncelle seul* (Paris: Éditions Salabert, [1929]). On Alexanian's relationship to Casals, see Falta, "A Great Wave," 6–14.
21. Igor Stravinsky and Robert Craft, *Themes and Episodes* (New York: Alfred A. Knopf, 1966), 102. The remarks attributed to Stravinsky were probably influenced by Craft.
22. Corredor, *Conversations with Casals*, 210.
23. Taruskin, "Six Times Six," 66.
24. Personal communication via teleconference, December 28, 2023.
25. See Anita Mercier, *Guilhermina Suggia: Cellist* (Aldershot: Ashgate Publishing, 2008). See Collins, "International Influence," 139–88.

26. Edwin Evans ("E. E."), review of British Women's Symphony Orchestra, *The Musical Times* 66, no. 985 (March 1, 1925): 256.
27. Anonymous ("C."), review of Wigmore Hall recital by Guilhermina Suggia and Vianna da Motta, *The Musical Times* 65, no. 982 (December 1, 1924): 1124.
28. For discographic details, see Mercier, *Guilhermina Suggia: Cellist*, 157.
29. Mercier, *Guilhermina Suggia: Cellist*, 56.
30. Amédée Daryl Williams, *Lillian Fuchs, First Lady of the Viola*, 2nd rev. ed. (Lincoln, NE: iUniverse Inc., 2004), 85–90.
31. Fuchs's recording is currently available as *Johann Sebastian Bach: Six Suites BWV 1007–1012* (Biddulph Recordings, 85002-2, 2021).
32. Howard Taubman, "Musicians' Guild Ends Fine Season," *The New York Times* (March 8, 1949): 31. Additional reviews are quoted in Williams, *Lillian Fuchs*, 88 and 91–94.
33. Louis Svećenski, *Johann Sebastian Bach: Six Suites for Violoncello, Adapted, Revised, and Fingered for Viola* (New York: G. Schirmer, 1916).
34. William Primrose, ed., *Johann Sebastian Bach, Five Suites for Viola* (New York: G. Schirmer, 1978). For further context on Fuchs's and Primrose's views of the Cello Suites on viola, see Williams, *Lillian Fuchs*, 95.
35. Anonymous ("C. J. L."), review of Lillian Fuchs, *J. S. Bach Suites Nos. 2 and 6*, *The American Record Guide* 18, no. 3 (November 1951): 84–85.
36. Williams, *Lillian Fuchs*, 91. I corroborated this anecdote with the violist Jeanne Mallow, who is Fuchs's granddaughter (personal communication, email dated January 1, 2024).
37. Ernst Kurth, ed., *Johann Sebastian Bach, Sechs Sonaten und sechs Suiten für Violine und Violoncello solo* (Munich: Drei Masken Verlag, 1921), xxi.
38. Ernst Kurth, *Grundlagen des Linearen Kontrapunkts: Einführung in Stil und Technik Bach's melodischer Polyphonie* (Bern: Max Dreschel, 1917), 224–25. For commentary, see Lee A. Rothfarb, *Ernst Kurth as Theorist and Analyst* (Philadelphia: University of Pennsylvania Press, 2016), 31–34.
39. Kurth, *Grundlagen*, 225–33.
40. Kurth, *Grundlagen*, 273; English translation in Kurth, *Ernst Kurth: Selected Writings*, trans. Lee Rothfarb (Cambridge: Cambridge University Press, 1991), 79–80. See also Rothfarb, *Ernst Kurth as Theorist and Analyst*, 82–83.
41. Heinrich Schenker, diary entry dated March 12, 1926, transcr. Marko Deislinger, trans. William Drabkin, www.schenkerdocumentsonline.org/documents/diaries/OJ-03-08_1926-03/r0012.html.

42. Heinrich Schenker, "The Sarabande of Bach's Suite No. 3 for Solo Violoncello," trans. Hedi Siegel, in *The Masterwork in Music: A Yearbook*, vol. 2, ed. William Drabkin (Mineola: Dover Publications, 2014), 55–58. This volume was originally published in 1927, although it is dated 1926.
43. Schenker, "The Sarabande of Bach's Suite No. 3," 58.
44. G. Hulshoff, *De zes suites voor violoncello-solo van Johann Sebastian Bach* (Arnhem: Van Loghum Slaterus, 1944). An English translation of the second edition (1962) was published in a small run as *The Six Suites for Violoncello Solo by Johann Sebastian Bach*, trans. Felix Douma (Port Rowan, ON: Leeboard Press, 1994) and includes a brief biographical sketch of the author. I am grateful to George Kennaway for drawing my attention to Hulshoff's book.
45. Anonymous, "Kunst: Het Soerabaiasch Kwartet," *De Indische Courant* 15, no. 161 (March 25, 1936): 14.
46. Hulshoff, *De zes suites voor violoncello-solo*, 101. Quotation translated by Shanti Nachtergaele.
47. Hulshoff, *De zes suites voor violoncello-solo*, 24–26.
48. Hulshoff, *De zes suites voor violoncello-solo*, 87–88. Quotation translated by Shanti Nachtergaele.
49. I thank Sumanth Gopinath for information about the Nokia preset ringtones (personal communication, email dated February 15, 2024).
50. Kenneth Furie, "Bach, a Cello, a Church in Burgundy, Rostropovich," *The New York Times* (June 18, 1995): 28H.
51. Yo-Yo Ma, *J. S. Bach: The 6 Unaccompanied Cello Suites* (CBS Masterworks, M2K37867, 2010). János Starker, *J. S. Bach: Suites for Solo Cello* (RCA Victor Red Seal, 09026-61436-2, 1997).
52. Anonymous, "Editorial Notes," *The Strad* 57, no. 692 (December 1947): 172.
53. Anonymous ("B. R."), "Henri Honegger: begaafd cellist," *Het Binnenhof* 4, no. 1203 (April 27, 1949): 3. Quotations translated by Shanti Nachtergaele.
54. Milly B. Stanfield, "Silhouettes from Britain," *Violins and Violinists Magazine* 18, no. 3 (May–June 1957): 101.
55. Anonymous ("G. v. L."), "Laatste Bach-matinee Orobio de Castro," *Het Binnenhof* 4, no. 1154 (February 28, 1949): 4. Quotation translated by Shanti Nachtergaele.
56. Anonymous ("B. R."), "Max Orobio de Castro speelt Bach," *Het Binnenhof* 4, no. 1118 (January 17, 1949): 5. Quotation translated by Shanti Nachtergaele.
57. Anonymous ("v. d. G."), "Orobio de Castro speelt Bach Tweede avond—Kleine Zaal," *Algemeen Handelsblad* 122, no. 39843 (April 12, 1949): 3. Quotation translated by Shanti Nachtergaele.

To the Present Day

58. For details, see concert listings in the *New Yorker* magazine.
59. Margery Bentwich, *Thelma Yellin: Pioneer Musician* (Jerusalem: Rubin Mass, 1964), 110.
60. Carlos Prieto, *The Adventures of a Cello*, trans. Elena C. Murray (Austin: University of Texas Press), 95–114.
61. Ma, *Six Evolutions: Bach Cello Suites* (Sony, 19075 85465 2, 2018). On *The Bach Project*, see http://bach.yo-yoma.com.
62. See the Bach in the Subways website, http://bachinthesubways.org.
63. Anonymous, "Uit Amsterdam," *Caecilia: Algemeen muzikaal tijdschrift van Nederland* 50, no. 25 (December 15, 1893): 209.
64. Annlies Schmidt, *J. S. Bach: Six Suites pour violoncelle seul* (Forgotten Records, FR118–19, 2009).
65. Nikolaus Harnoncourt, *J. S. Bach: Cello Suites, BWV 1007–1012* (Apex, 2564 608816-2, 2003). Anner Bylsma, *J. S. Bach: Six Cello Suites* (Sony Classical, SB2K60880, 1999).
66. Sigiswald Kuijken's recording on viola da spalla is *Bach Cello Suites* (Accent, ACC24196, 2009).
67. François Rabbath, *Bach, Suites pour violoncelle seul à la contrebasse* (Disques du Solstice, SOCD292-93, 2012). Richard Hartshorne, *J. S. Bach: Six Solo Suites* (Centaur Records, CRC2348–50, 1997). Edgar Meyer, *Bach: Unaccompanied Cello Suites* (Sony Classical, SK89183, 2000).
68. On bass transcriptions, see Andrew Kohn, "Bach Cello Suites for the Bass: The State of the Research," *Música hodie* 9, no. 1 (2009): 11–30.
69. Amy Porter, *In Translation: Selections from J. S. Bach's Cello Suites* (Equilibrium Records, EQ124, 2013).
70. Peter Crocker, *Bach Cello Suites Arranged for Trombone* ([no label information], 2021).
71. Fernando Meza, *Suites for Unaccompanied Cello Performed on Marimba* ([no label information], 2006). Gwendolyn Burgett Thrasher, *Marimba Suites* (Blue Griffin, 2007). See also Nathan David Tingler, "Bach and the Marimba: Bridging the Gap to Non-Percussionists" (DMA diss., University of Georgia, 2020).
72. Yamashita Kazuhito, *J. S. Bach: The Complete Suites for Solo Cello, Guitar Version* (Crown Classics, CRCC8003-4, 1993). Andreas von Wangenheim, *J. S. Bach: Six Suites for Violoncello Solo (Transcription for Guitar)* (Arte Nova Classics, ANO675220, 1999).
73. Paolo Pandolfo, *Bach: The Six Suites* (Glossa, GCD920405, 2001).
74. Michael J. Miles, *American Bach* (Right Turn on Red Music, 822, 1997); and Miles, *American Bach Revisited* (Right Turn on Red Music, 1311, 2023).
75. Thomas Preece, arr., *Selections from the Bach Cello Suites, Arranged for Ukulele* (self-published, 2015).

76. Rachel Podger, *J. S. Bach: Cello Suites* (Channel Classics, SA41119, 2019). Johnny Gandelsman, *J. S. Bach: Complete Cello Suites* (In a Circle Records, ICR013, 2020). Jorge Jiménez, *Rethinking Bach: The Cello Suites* (Pan Classics, PC10434, 2022). Tomás Cotik, *Bach: The Six Suites* (Centaur, CRC4030–31, 2024).
77. See Sunhaeng Lee, "The Legacy of Bach's Cello Suites in Twentieth-Century Solo Cello Suites," DMA diss., University of Cincinnati, 2020. See also Robin Stowell, "Other Solo Repertory," in *The Cambridge Companion to the Cello*, ed. Robin Stowell (Cambridge: Cambridge University Press, 1999), 137–45.
78. Peter Gregson, *Bach: The Cello Suites Recomposed by Peter Gregson* (Deutsche Grammophon, 53037372, 2018).
79. Mike Block and Barry Rothman, *Step into the Void* (Bright Shiny Things, BSTC0132, 2020). Block has also recorded videos of the complete Cello Suites "performed in acoustically glorious bathrooms of the finest concert halls" (Bach in the Bathroom, www.bachinthebathroom.com).
80. Julia MacLaine, *Preludes* (Analekta, AN28914, 2022).
81. Full details are available on Alisa Weilerstein's website at http://alisaweilerstein.com/fragments.
82. Yo-Yo Ma, *The Cello Suites: Inspired by Bach* (Sony Classical, S2K63203, 1997).
83. Yo-Yo Ma, *The Cello Suites: Inspired by Bach* [films] (Sony Classical, SV3D58785, 2004). See also David Bartine, "Contrapuntal Invention in *Six Gestures*: Reading J. S. Bach's Sixth Suite for Unaccompanied Cello on Film," *Interdisciplinary Literary Studies* 13, nos. 1–2 (Fall 2011): 178–99.
84. Martin Goodman, *The Cellist of Dachau* (London: Barbican Press, 2023). Melanie Heuiser Hill, *Giant Pumpkin Suite* (Somerville: Candlewick Press, 2017). Mark Moskowitz, *The Eyes of Bach* (Altona: Friesen Press, 2024).
85. Gary Gildner, "The Bach Cello Suites," *The Antioch Review* 72, no. 2 (Spring 2014): 261–69. David Janisch, "The Cello in the Cell," *Nightmare Magazine* 133 (October 2023), www.nightmare-magazine.com/fiction/the-cello-in-the-cell.
86. Examples include Judith Glyde, *Under the Goddess of the Sky: A Journey through Solitude, Bach, and the Himalayas* (Kenmore: Coffeetown Press, 2024); Eric Siblin, *The Cello Suites: J. S. Bach, Pablo Casals, and the Search for a Baroque Masterpiece* (New York: Atlantic Monthly Press, 2009); and Miranda Wilson, *The Well-Tempered Cello: Life with Bach Cello Suites* (Austin: Fairhaven Press, 2022).
87. Douglas R. Hofstadter, *Gödel, Escher, Bach: An Eternal Golden Braid* (New York: Basic Books, 1979), 69–71 and 78–79.

88. Martin Jarvis, *Written by Mrs Bach* (Sydney: HarperCollins, 2011). Jarvis's (widely discredited) speculation that the Cello Suites were composed by Anna Magdalena Bach is rooted in a misunderstanding of the distinction between *écrite* ("written") and *composée* ("composed") on the title page of Source A. See Ruth Tatlow, "A Missed Opportunity: Reflections on *Written by Mrs Bach*," *Understanding Bach* 10 (March 2015): 141–57; and Talle, "Who Was Anna Magdalena Bach?," 144–49.
89. Ursula K. Le Guin, *The Hainish Novels & Stories*, vol. 2 (New York: Library of America, 2017), xviii.
90. Personal communication with Wendy Sutter, email dated March 6, 2024.
91. On the Bach prelude in *The Pianist* and *Master and Commander*, see Lawrence Kramer, *Why Classical Music Still Matters* (Berkeley: University of California Press, 2009), 26–29.
92. Mervyn Cooke, *A History of Film Music* (Cambridge: Cambridge University Press, 2008), 450. See also Olga Haldey, "Voice of the Dance: J. S. Bach and Other Classics in the Maksimova-Vasiliev Film *Fouetté* (1986)," *BACH* 50, no. 2 (2019): 149.
93. Per F. Broman, "Another Woody: J. S. Bach in Dixieland," *BACH* 50, no. 2 (2019): 259–62.
94. Kevin Shihoten, "Cellist Performs atop Mt. Fuji," *Playbill*, June 19, 2007, www.playbill.com/article/cellist-performs-atop-mt-fuji. The Italian videos are available on YouTube.
95. See Tristan Cook's documentary *Strangers on the Earth* (Walk to Fisterra, 2016).
96. "Luka Šulić Plays Cello in the Snowy Monte Canin," *In Trieste*, June 7, 2020, www.intrieste.com/2020/06/07/luka-sulic-plays-cello-in-the-snowy-monte-canin.
97. Gavin Carver, "Andante," Vimeo video, uploaded August 20, 2014, http://vimeo.com/103919788.
98. See also Glyde's memoir *Under the Goddess of the Sky* about her experience studying the Cello Suites intensively in a secluded setting in the Himalayas.
99. Heike Hoffer, "Aesthetics of Destruction: Music and the Worldview of Ikari Shinji in *Neon Genesis Evangelion*" (MM thesis, University of Arizona, 2012), 75–76.
100. Paul Kupfer, "'Good Hands': The Music of J. S. Bach in Television Commercials," *BACH* 50, no. 2 (2019): 278–81.
101. Alisa Weilerstein, *Bach* (Pentatone, PTC5186751, 2020).

BIBLIOGRAPHY

Adlung, Jakob. *Anleitung zu der musikalischen Gelahrtheit*. Erfurt, 1758.
Alexanian, Diran, ed. *J. S. Bach, Six Suites pour violoncelle seul*. Paris: Éditions Salabert, [1929].
Anonymous. Concert advertisement. *Écho des Pyrénées* 6, no. 864 (November 26, 1879): no pagination.
Anonymous. Concert advertisement. *Écho des Pyrénées* 8, no. 1046 (January 19, 1881): no pagination.
Anonymous. Concert advertisement. *L'Industriel alsacien: Journal de l'industrie* 32, no. 100 (November 22, 1866): no pagination.
Anonymous. "Concerts et auditions musicales." *Revue et gazette musicale* 42, no. 6 (February 7, 1875): 45–46.
Anonymous. "Editorial Notes." *The Strad* 57, no. 692 (December 1947): 171–73.
Anonymous. "Kunst: Het Soerabaiasch Kwartet." *De Indische Courant* 15, no. 161 (March 25, 1936): 14.
Anonymous. "Metropolitan Examinations of the Royal Academy of Music." *The Musical Standard* 21, no. 903 (November 19, 1881): 322–23.
Anonymous. "Music from Abroad." *Dwight's Journal of Music* 24, no. 24 (February 18, 1865): 396–98.
Anonymous. "Musique de piano." *Le Ménestrel* 70, no. 44 (October 30, 1904): 345.
Anonymous. "Nouvelles diverses." *Le Ménestrel* 30, no. 51 (November 22, 1863): 410.
Anonymous. Review of Altenburg *Singakademie* concert. *Neue Zeitschrift für Musik* 63, no. 48 (November 22, 1867): 425.
Anonymous. Review of Altenburg *Singakademie* concert. *Neue Zeitschrift für Musik* 64, no. 49 (November 27, 1868): 424.
Anonymous. Review of *Gavotte en ré de John [sic] Sebastian Bach, transcrite pour piano par D. Brocca*. *The Musical World* 48, no. 48 (November 26, 1870): 789.
Anonymous. Review of Monday Popular Concert. *The Musical World* 46, no. 2 (January 11, 1868): 19.
Anonymous. Review of Saturday Popular Concert. *The Athenæum* 3399 (December 17, 1892): 864.
Anonymous. Review of various editions of Bach's music. *The Musical World* 8 (1838): 260–63.

Bibliography

Anonymous. "Société J.-S. Bach." *La revue musicale* 5, no. 20 (November 1, 1905): 528.
Anonymous. "Uit Amsterdam." *Caecilia: Algemeen muzikaal tijdschrift van Nederland* 50, no. 25 (December 15, 1893): 209.
Anonymous ("A. R."). Review of Julius Klengel and E. Steinberger, Sarabande in D Major (Bach) and Adagio cantabile in G Major (Tartini). *The Gramophone* 14, no. 159 (August 1936): 112.
Anonymous ("B. R."). "Henri Honegger: begaafd cellist." *Het Binnenhof* 4, no. 1203 (April 27, 1949): 3.
"Max Orobio de Castro speelt Bach." *Het Binnenhof* 4, no. 1118 (January 17, 1949): 5.
Anonymous ("C."). Review of Wigmore Hall recital by Guilhermina Suggia and Vianna da Motta. *The Musical Times* 65, no. 982 (December 1, 1924): 1124.
Anonymous ("C. J. L."). Review of Lillian Fuchs, *J. S. Bach Suites Nos. 2 and 6*. *The American Record Guide* 18, no. 3 (November 1951): 84–85.
Anonymous ("G. v. L."). "Laatste Bach-matinee Orobio de Castro." *Het Binnenhof* 4, no. 1154 (February 28, 1949): 4.
Anonymous ("M."). Concert review. *La Réforme* 14, no. 261 (September 18, 1897): no pagination.
Anonymous ("R. S."). Review of Sixth Euterpe Concert. *Musikalisches Wochenblatt* 1, no. 5 (January 28, 1870): 74.
Anonymous ("S. R."). "Correspondenz: Dresden." *Neue Zeitschrift für Musik* 63, no. 20 (May 10, 1867): 177–78.
Anonymous ("V."). Items received from Merseburger Verlag. *The Violin Times: A Monthly Journal for Professional and Amateur Violinists and Quartet Players* 3, no. 35 (September 15, 1896): 43.
Anonymous ("v. d. G."). "Orobio de Castro speelt Bach Tweede avond—Kleine Zaal." *Algemeen Handelsblad* 122, no. 39843 (April 12, 1949): 3.
Arnold, Yourij von [Yuri Karlovich Arnold]. "Correspondenz: Leipzig" (review of First Euterpe Concert). *Neue Zeitschrift für Musik* 60, no. 45 (November 4, 1864): 396.
"Correspondenz: Leipzig." *Neue Zeitschrift für Musik* 61, no. 2 (January 6, 1865): 10–11.
Bach, C. P. E. *Essay on the True Art of Playing Keyboard Instruments*. Translated and edited by William J. Mitchell. New York: W. W. Norton, 1949.
Verzeichniß des musikalischen Nachlasses des verstorbenen Capellmeisters Carl Philipp Emanuel Bach. Hamburg, 1790.
Badiarov, Dmitry. "The Violoncello, Viola da Spalla and Viola Pomposa in Theory and Practice." *The Galpin Society Journal* 60 (April 2007): 121–45.
Bandy, Dorian. "Violin Technique and the Contrapuntal Imagination in 17th-Century German Lands." *Early Music* 49, no. 2 (May 2021): 275–91.
Barnett, Gregory. "The Violoncello da Spalla: Shouldering the Cello in the Baroque Era." *Journal of the American Musical Instrument Society* 24 (1998): 81–106.

Bibliography

Barré, Martin. "Casals, Discoverer of Bach's Cello Suites?" Paper presented at "Casals 50: Romantique ou moderne?," Maison Heinrich Heine, Paris, November 16, 2023.

———. "La Fabrique du canon: Les Suites pour violoncelle de Bach avant Pablo Casals." *Mémoire en esthétique* document. Conservatoire national supérieur de musique et de danse de Paris, 2023. http://mediatheque.cnsmdp.fr. SyrtisID 39617013.

Bartel, Dietrich. *Musica Poetica: Musical-Rhetorical Figures in German Baroque Music*. Lincoln, NE: University of Nebraska Press, 1997.

Bartine, David. "Contrapuntal Invention in *Six Gestures*: Reading J. S. Bach's Sixth Suite for Unaccompanied Cello on Film." *Interdisciplinary Literary Studies* 13, nos. 1–2 (Fall 2011): 178–99.

Becker, Hugo, ed. *Sechs Suiten (Sonaten) für Violoncello solo von Joh. Seb. Bach*. Leipzig: C. F. Peters, [1890].

Becker, Hugo, and Dago Rynar. *Mechanik und Ästhetik des Violoncellspiels*. Vienna and Leipzig: Universal Edition, 1929.

Bennett, Joseph. "'Thaddeus Egg' Identified!" *The Musical Times and Singing Class Circular* 41, no. 683 (January 1, 1900): 52.

Bentwich, Margery. *Thelma Yellin: Pioneer Musician*. Jerusalem: Rubin Mass, 1964.

Bernstein, Chelsea. "Bach's Cello Suites and the French Bass Viol Tradition." DMA diss., University of Maryland, 2020.

Blackman, Paul. *Christian Reimers: A Spirited Performer*. Campbelltown, NSW: Paul Blackman, 2017.

Block, Mike, and Barry Rothman. *Step into the Void*. Bright Shiny Things, BSTC0132, 2020.

Brody, Christopher. "Second-Reprise Opening Schemas in Bach's Binary Movements." *Music Theory Spectrum* 43, no. 2 (Fall 2021): 257–79.

Broman, Per F. "Another Woody: J. S. Bach in Dixieland." *BACH* 50, no. 2 (2019): 254–74.

Bunge, Rudolf. "Johann Sebastian Bachs Kapelle zu Cöthen und deren nachgelassene Instrumente." *Bach-Jahrbuch* 2 (1905): 14–47.

Burgett Thrasher, Gwendolyn. *Marimba Suites*. Blue Griffin, 2007.

Butt, John. "Bach and the Dance of Humankind." In *Musicology and Dance: Historical and Critical Perspectives*, edited by Davinia Caddy and Maribeth Clark, 19–48. Cambridge: Cambridge University Press, 2020.

———. *Bach's Dialogue with Modernity: Perspectives on the Passions*. Cambridge: Cambridge University Press, 2010.

Bylsma, Anner. *Bach, the Fencing Master: About Mrs. Anna Magdalena Bach's Autograph Copy of the 6 Suites for Violoncello Solo senza Basso of Johann Sebastian Bach*. Rev. ed. Amsterdam: The Fencing Mail, 2019.

———. *J. S. Bach: Six Cello Suites*. Sony Classical, SB2K60880, 1999.

Bibliography

Campbell, Margaret. "Masters of the Twentieth Century." In *The Cambridge Companion to the Cello*, edited by Robin Stowell, 73–91. Cambridge: Cambridge University Press, 1999.

———. "Nineteenth-Century Virtuosi." In *The Cambridge Companion to the Cello*, edited by Robin Stowell, 61–72. Cambridge: Cambridge University Press, 1999.

Casals, Pablo. *Encores and Transcriptions*. Vol. 2, *1927–30*. Naxos, 8.110976, 2004.

———. *Joys and Sorrows: Reflections by Pablo Casals as Told to Albert E. Kahn*. London: MacDonald and Co., 1970.

Chambers, Mark. "The 'Mistuned' Cello: Precursors to J. S. Bach's Suite V in C Minor for Unaccompanied Violoncello." DMA diss., Florida State University, 1996.

Choron, Alexandre-Étienne, and François-Joseph-Marie Fayole. *Dictionnaire historique des musiciens*. 2 vols. Paris, 1810–11.

Collins, Hannah E. "International Influence on the Development of Cello Playing in England, 1870–1930: Robert Hausmann, August Van Biene, and Guilhermina Suggia." DMA diss., CUNY Graduate Center, 2020.

Cook, Tristan. *Strangers on the Earth*. New York: Walk to Fisterra, 2016.

Cooke, Mervyn. *A History of Film Music*. Cambridge: Cambridge University Press, 2008.

Corredor, J. Ma. *Conversations with Casals*. Translated by André Mangeot. New York: E. P. Button & Co., 1957.

Cotik, Tomás. *Bach: The Six Suites*. Centaur, CRC4030-31, 2024.

Crocker, Peter. *Bach Cello Suites Arranged for Trombone*. [No label information], 2021.

David, Ferdinand, arr. *Sechs Suiten für die Violine solo von Joh. Seb. Bach: Als Vorstudien zu den grossen Violin-Sonaten dieses Meisters [. . .]*. Leipzig: Gustav Heinze, [1866].

David, Hans T., and Arthur Mendel, eds. *The Bach Reader: A Life of Johann Sebastian Bach in Letters and Documents*. Rev. ed. New York: W. W. Norton, 1972.

David, Hans T., Arthur Mendel, and Christoph Wolff, eds. *The New Bach Reader: A Life of Johann Sebastian Bach in Letters and Documents*. New York: W. W. Norton, 1998.

Delpech, Louis. "Les Musiciens français en Allemagne du nord (1660–1730): Questions de méthode." *Diasporas* 26 (2015). http://doi.org/10.4000/diasporas.406.

Dörffel, Alfred, ed. *Johann Sebastian Bach's Kammermusik, Vol. 6, Solowerke für Violine, Solowerke für Violoncello*. Leipzig: Breitkopf & Härtel, [1879].

D'Ortigue, J. Review of chamber music concert organized by Alfred Holmes. *Journal du débats politiques et littéraires*, January 26, 1866: no pagination.

Dotzauer, J. J. F. *Méthode de violoncelle*. Mayence, [1823].

Bibliography

Six Solos ou études pour le violoncelle, ouvrage posthume. Leipzig: Breitkopf & Härtel, [1826].

Drönewolf, Otto. "Die Tonkünstler-Versammlung zu Meiningen." *Neue Zeitschrift für Musik* 63, no. 40 (September 27, 1867): 345–48.

Egg, Thaddeus [Joseph Bennett]. "Charles Hallé's Pianoforte Recitals." *The Musical World* 51, no. 23 (June 7, 1873): 374.

Eisel, Johann Philipp. *Musicus Autodidaktos*. Erfurt, 1738.

Eisenberg, Maurice. "Casals and the Bach Suites." *The New York Times*, October 10, 1943: X7.

Ellis, Katharine. *Interpreting the Musical Past: Early Music in Nineteenth-Century France*. Oxford: Oxford University Press, 2008.

——— . *Music Criticism in Nineteenth-Century France: La Revue et gazette musicale de Paris 1834–80*. Cambridge: Cambridge University Press, 1995.

Evans, Edwin ("E. E."). Review of British Women's Symphony Orchestra. *The Musical Times* 66, no. 985 (March 1, 1925): 256.

Fabian, Dorottya. "Towards a Performance History of Bach's Sonatas and Partitas for Solo Violin: Preliminary Investigations." In *Essays in Honor of László Somfai on His 70th Birthday: Studies in the Sources and the Interpretation of Music*, edited by Laszlo Vikárius and Vera Lampert, 87–108. Lanham, MD: Scarecrow Press, 2005.

Falta, Oskar. "A Great Wave in the Evolution of the Modern Cellist: Diran Alexanian and Maurice Eisenberg, Two Master Cello Pedagogues from the Legacy of Pablo Casals." DMA diss., University of British Columbia, 2019.

Fanselau, Clemens. *Mehrstimmigkeit in J. S. Bachs Werken für Melodieinstrumente ohne Begleitung*. Berlin: Schewe, 2000.

Fauchier-Magnan, Adrien. *The Small German Courts in the Eighteenth Century*. Translated by Mervyn Savill. London: Methuen, 1958.

Fayet, L. F. R., and B. Dutertre, eds. "Musique instrumentale." *Journal générale d'annonce des œuvres de musique, gravures, lithographies, etc. publiés en France et à l'étranger* 1, no. 16 (April 22, 1825): 127–28.

Field, Elizabeth I. "Performing Solo Bach: An Examination of the Evolution of Performance Traditions of Bach's Unaccompanied Violin Sonatas from 1802 to the Present." DMA diss., Cornell University, 1999.

Fock, Gustav. *Der junge Bach in Lüneburg: 1700 bis 1702*. Hamburg: Merseburger Verlag, 1950.

Framery, Nicolas-Étienne, et al., eds. *Encyclopédie méthodique: Musique*. 2 vols. Paris, 1791–1818.

Friedrich II of Prussia. *Memoires pour servir à l'histoire de la Maison de Brandebourg*. 2 vols. Berlin, 1751.

Fuchs, Lillian. *Johann Sebastian Bach: Six Suites BWV 1007–1012*. Biddulph Recordings, 85002–2, 2021.

Fuhrmann, Martin Heinrich. *Musicalischer-Trichter*. Frankfurt, 1706.

Bibliography

Fuller, David. "Suite." In *Grove Music Online*, edited by Deane Root. Published January 20, 2001.

Furie, Kenneth. "Bach, a Cello, a Church in Burgundy, Rostropovich." *The New York Times*, June 18, 1995: 28H.

Gandelsman, Johnny. *J. S. Bach: Complete Cello Suites*. In a Circle Records, ICR013, 2020.

Geck, Martin. *Johann Sebastian Bach: Life and Work*. Translated by John Hargraves. Orlando: Harcourt, 2006.

Geiringer, Karl, and Irene Geiringer. *The Bach Family: Seven Generations of Creative Genius*. Oxford: Oxford University Press, 1954.

Gerber, Ernst Ludwig. *Historisch-Biographisches Lexikon der Tonkünstler*. 2 vols. Leipzig, 1790–92.

Neues Historisch-Biographisches Lexikon der Tonkünstler. 4 vols. Leipzig, 1812–14.

Gildner, Gary. "The Bach Cello Suites." *The Antioch Review* 72, no. 2 (Spring 2014): 261–69.

Giles, Anna Benson. *Pau Casals*. London: BBC TV, 1991.

Glyde, Judith. *Under the Goddess of the Sky: A Journey through Solitude, Bach, and the Himalayas*. Kenmore: Coffeetown Press, 2024.

Goodman, Martin. *The Cellist of Dachau*. London: Barbican Press, 2023.

Göthel, Folker, and Peter Wollny. "Westhoff, Johann Paul von." In *Grove Music Online*, edited by Deane Root. Published January 20, 2001.

Grädener, Carl G. P., arr. *Sechs Sonaten für das Violoncell von Joh. Seb. Bach mit Klavierbegleitung*. 2 vols. Hamburg: H. Pohle, [1871].

Grant, Roger Matthew. *Beating Time & Measuring Music in the Early Modern Era*. Oxford: Oxford University Press, 2014.

Greenberg, Yoel. *How Sonata Forms: A Bottom-Up Approach to Musical Form*. Oxford: Oxford University Press, 2022.

Gregson, Peter. *Bach: The Cello Suites Recomposed by Peter Gregson*. Deutsche Grammophon, 53037372, 2018.

Grier, James. *The Critical Editing of Music: History, Method, and Practice*. Cambridge: Cambridge University Press, 1996.

Grützmacher, Friedrich, ed. *Sechs Suiten (Sonaten) für Violoncello solo von Joh. Seb. Bach, Original-Ausgabe*. Leipzig: C. F. Peters, [1867].

Six Sonates ou suites pour violoncelle seul par J. Seb. Bach. Édition nouvelle, revue et arrangée pour être exécuté aux concerts par Fr. Grützmacher. Leipzig: C. F. Peters, [1866].

Haimovitz, Matt. *J. S. Bach: The Cello Suites According to Anna Magdalena*. Pentatone, PTC5186555, 2015.

Haldey, Olga. "Voice of the Dance: J. S. Bach and Other Classics in the Maksimova-Vasiliev Film *Fouetté* (1986)." *BACH* 50, no. 2 (2019): 136–74.

Harnoncourt, Nikolaus. *J. S. Bach: Cello Suites, BWV 1007–1012*. Apex, 2564 608816-2, 2003.

Bibliography

Hartshorne, Richard. *J. S. Bach: Six Solo Suites*. Centaur Records, CRC2348–50, 1997.
Harvey, Keith, ed. *The Recorded Cello: The History of the Cello on Record*. Vol. 2. Pearl, GEMM9984–86, 1992.
Heinze, Sara, arr. *Bach-Album: A Collection of Twenty-One Favorite Pieces for Pianoforte by Johann Sebastian Bach*. New York, 1898.
  Bach-Album: Beliebte Stücke für Pianoforte Solo von Joh. Seb. Bach. Rev. ed. Leipzig, [1878].
Hill, Melanie Heuiser. *Giant Pumpkin Suite*. Somerville: Candlewick Press, 2017.
Ho, Joanna, and Teresa Martinez. *Playing at the Border: A Story of Yo-Yo Ma*. Fairfax: Literary Ideas, 2021.
Hoffer, Heike. "Aesthetics of Destruction: Music and the Worldview of Ikari Shinji in *Neon Genesis Evangelion*." MM thesis, University of Arizona, 2012.
Hofstadter, Douglas R. *Gödel, Escher, Bach: An Eternal Golden Braid*. New York: Basic Books, 1979.
Holoman, D. Kern. *The Société des Concerts du Conservatoire, 1828–1967*. Berkeley: University of California Press, 2004.
Hulshoff, G. *De zes suites voor violoncello-solo van Johann Sebastian Bach*. Arnhem: Van Loghum Slaterus, 1944. Translated by Felix Douma as *The Six Suites for Violoncello Solo by Johann Sebastian Bach*. Port Rowan, ON: Leeboard Press, 1994.
Isserlis, Steven. *The Bach Cello Suites: A Companion*. London: Faber & Faber, 2021.
Janisch, David. "The Cello in the Cell." *Nightmare Magazine* 133 (October 2023). www.nightmare-magazine.com/fiction/the-cello-in-the-cell.
Janof, Tim. "Conversation with Bernard Greenhouse (November, 1998)." Cello Bello. Accessed January 1, 2024. www.cellobello.org/cello-blog/internet-cello-society-archive/conversation-with-bernard-greenhouse.
Jarvis, Martin. *Written by Mrs Bach*. Sydney: HarperCollins, 2011.
Jiménez, Jorge. *Rethinking Bach: The Cello Suites*. Pan Classics, PC10434, 2022.
Kelley, Edgar Stillman. "The Unpublished Bach-Schumann Violoncello Suites." *Music: A Monthly Magazine* 3, no. 6 (April 1893): 611–19.
Kennaway, George. "Bach Solo Cello Suites: An Overview of Editions." CHASE. Accessed January 1, 2024. http://mhm.hud.ac.uk/chase/article/bach-solo-cello-suites-an-overview-of-editions-george-kennaway (site discontinued).
  Playing the Cello, 1780–1930. New York: Routledge, 2016.
Kirk, H. L. *Pablo Casals: A Biography*. New York: Holt, Rinehart, and Winston, 1974.
Kirnberger, Johann Philipp. *Die Kunst des reinen Satzes in der Musik*. 2 vols. Berlin and Königsberg, 1774–79.
  Recueil d'airs de danse caractéristiques. Berlin, c. 1777.
Klengel, Julius. *Julius Klengel: A Celebration*. Cello Classics, CC1024, 2012.

Bibliography

Klengel, Julius, ed. *J. S. Bach Sechs Suiten für Violoncell*. Leipzig: Breitkopf & Härtel, [1900].

Knobel, Bradley. "Bach Cello Suites with Piano Accompaniment and Nineteenth-Century Bach Discovery." DMA diss., Florida State University, 2006.

Kohn, Andrew. "Bach Cello Suites for the Bass: The State of the Research." *Música hodie* 9, no. 1 (2009): 11–30.

Köpp, Kai. "Vom Ensemble- zum Soloinstrument: Das Violoncello." In *Bachs Orchester- und Kammermusik: Das Handbuch*, 2 vols., edited by Siegbert Rampe, 2:253–63. Laaber: Laaber Verlag, 2013.

Kramer, Lawrence. *Why Classical Music Still Matters*. Berkeley: University of California Press, 2009.

Kuijken, Sigiswald. *Bach Cello Suites*. Accent, ACC24196, 2009.

Kupfer, Paul. "'Good Hands': The Music of J. S. Bach in Television Commercials." *BACH* 50, no. 2 (2019): 275–302.

Kurth, Ernst. *Ernst Kurth: Selected Writings*. Translated by Lee Rothfarb. Cambridge: Cambridge University Press, 1991.

——— . *Grundlagen des Linearen Kontrapunkts: Einführung in Stil und Technik Bach's melodischer Polyphonie*. Bern: Max Dreschel, 1917.

Kurth, Ernst, ed. *Johann Sebastian Bach, Sechs Sonaten und sechs Suiten für Violine und Violoncello solo*. Munich: Drei Masken Verlag, 1921.

Laloy, Louis ("L. L."). "Résultats des concours." *Bulletin français de la Société international de musique* 5, nos. 8–9 (July 15, 1909): 763–84.

Lawson, Colin, and Robin Stowell. *The Historical Performance of Music: An Introduction*. Cambridge: Cambridge University Press, 1999.

Le Blanc, Hubert. *Défense de la basse de viole contre les entréprises du violon et les prétentions du violoncel*. Amsterdam, 1740.

Ledbetter, David. *Unaccompanied Bach: Performing the Solo Works*. New Haven: Yale University Press, 2009.

Lee, Meebae. "Rewriting the Past, Composing the Future: Schumann and the Rediscovery of Bach." PhD diss., CUNY Graduate Center, 2011.

Lee, Sunhaeng. "The Legacy of Bach's Cello Suites in Twentieth-Century Solo Cello Suites." DMA diss., University of Cincinnati, 2020.

Legge, Robin H. "Music for the Violoncello." *Musical Opinion and Music Trade Review* 16, no. 186 (March 1893): 353.

Le Guin, Ursula K. *The Hainish Novels & Stories*. Vol. 2. New York: Library of America, 2017.

Leisinger, Ulrich. "Bachian Fugues in Mozart's Vienna." *Bach Notes: The Newsletter of the American Bach Society* 6 (Fall 2006): 1–7.

——— . Commentary to *Suites for Violoncello Solo*, by Johann Sebastian Bach. 5th ed. Vienna: Wiener Urtext, 2000.

Lester, Joel. *Bach's Works for Solo Violin: Style, Structure, Performance*. Oxford: Oxford University Press, 1999.

Bibliography

"J. S. Bach Teaches Us How to Compose: Four Pattern Preludes from the *Well-Tempered Clavier.*" *College Music Symposium* 38 (1998): 33–46.

"Reading and Misreading: Schumann's Accompaniments to Bach's Sonatas and Partitas for Solo Violin." *Current Musicology* 56 (1994): 24–53.

Liégois, C., and E. Nogué. *Le Violoncelle: Son histoire, ses virtuoses.* Paris: Constallat & Cie, [1913].

Little, Meredith, and Natalie Jenne. *Dance and the Music of J. S. Bach.* Bloomington: Indiana University Press, 1991.

Little, Meredith Ellis. "Gavotte." In *Grove Music Online*, revised by Matthew Werley, edited by Deane Root. Published January 20, 2001; revised September 3, 2014.

Lützen, Ludolf. *Die Violoncell-Transkriptionen Friedrich Grützmachers: Untersuchung zur Transkription in Sicht und Handhabung der 2. Hälfte des 19. Jahrhunderts.* Regensburg: Gustav Bosse, 1974.

Ma, Yo-Yo. *The Cello Suites: Inspired by Bach.* Sony Classical, S2K63203, 1997.

The Cello Suites: Inspired by Bach [films]. Sony Classical, SV3D58785, 2004.

J. S. Bach: The 6 Unaccompanied Cello Suites. CBS Masterworks, M2K37867, 2010.

Six Evolutions: Bach Cello Suites. Sony, 19075 85465 2, 2018.

Mace, Thomas. *Musick's Monument; or, A Remembrancer of the Best Practical Musick.* London, 1676.

MacGregor, Lynda. "Norblin (de la Gourdaine), Louis (Pierre Martin)." In *Grove Music Online*, edited by Deane Root. Published January 20, 2001.

Machy, Sieur de. *Pièces de violle.* Paris, 1685.

MacLaine, Julia. *Preludes.* Analekta, AN28914, 2022.

Maclean, Charles. "[Leipzig] Bach Festival Impressions." *The Musical Times* 45, no. 741 (November 1, 1904): 733–35.

Majer, Joseph Friedrich Bernhard Caspar. *Neu-eröffnete theoretisch und pracktischer Music-Saal.* Nuremberg, 1741.

Markevitch, Dimitry. *Cello Story.* Translated by Florence W. Seder. Princeton: Summy-Birchard Music, 1984.

Marshall, Robert L. "Toward a Twenty-First-Century Bach Biography." *Musical Quarterly* 84, no. 3 (Autumn 2000): 497–525.

Marshall, Robert L., and Traute M. Marshall. *Exploring the World of J. S. Bach: A Traveler's Guide.* Urbana: University of Illinois Press, 2016.

Mattheson, Johann. *Das neu-eröffnete Orchester.* Hamburg, 1713.

Johann Mattheson's "Der vollkommene Capellmeister": A Revised Translation with Critical Commentary. Translated by Ernest Charles Harriss. Ann Arbor: UMI Research Press, 1981.

McCreless, Patrick. "The Pitch-Class Motive in Tonal Analysis: Some Historical and Critical Observations." *Res Musica* 3 (2011): 52–68.

McKee, Eric. *Decorum of the Minuet, Delirium of the Waltz: A Study of Dance-Music Relations in 3/4 Time.* Bloomington: Indiana University Press, 2013.

Bibliography

Mendel, Émile. "Nouvelles des théâtres." *Paris-Journal* 6, no. 30 (January 31, 1873): 3.
Mercier, Anita. *Guilhermina Suggia: Cellist.* Aldershot: Ashgate Publishing, 2008.
Méreaux, Amédée. "Tablettes du pianiste et du chanteur: Les Clavecinistes (de 1637 à 1790)." *Le Ménestrel* 30, no. 51 (November 22, 1863): 408–9.
Mersenne, Marin. *Harmonie universelle.* 2 vols. Paris, 1636–37.
Meyer, Edgar. *Bach: Unaccompanied Cello Suites.* Sony Classical, SK89183, 2000.
Meza, Fernando. *Suites for Unaccompanied Cello Performed on Marimba.* [No label information], 2006.
Miles, Michael J. *American Bach.* Right Turn on Red Music, 822, 1997.
———. *American Bach Revisited.* Right Turn on Red Music, 1311, 2023.
Moskowitz, Mark. *The Eyes of Bach.* Altona: Friesen Press, 2024.
Mozart, Leopold. *A Treatise on the Fundamental Principles of Violin Playing.* 2nd ed. Translated by Editha Knocker. Oxford: Oxford University Press, 1951.
Murr, Christoph Gottlieb von. *Journal zur Kunstgeschichte und zur allgemeinen Litteratur, Zweyter Theil.* Nuremberg, 1776.
Ng, Shaun Kam Fook. "Le Sieur de Machy and the French Solo Viol Tradition." MA thesis, University of Western Australia, 2008.
Niedt, Friedrich Erhard. *The Musical Guide: Parts I (1700/10), II (1721), and III (1717).* Translated by Pamela L. Poulin and Irmgard C. Taylor. Oxford: Clarendon Press, 1989.
Norblin, Louis-Pierre, ed. *Six Sonates ou études pour le violoncelle composées par J. Sébastien Bach, œuvre posthume.* Paris: Janet et Cotelle, [1824].
Owens, Samantha, Barbara M. Reul, and Janice B. Stockigt, eds. *Music at German Courts, 1715–1760: Changing Artistic Priorities.* Woodbridge: Boydell & Brewer, 2012.
Pandolfo, Paolo. *Bach: The Six Suites.* Glossa, GCD920405, 2001.
Pauer, Ernst. "The Pianoforte Teacher: A Collection of Articles Intended for Educational Purposes." *Monthly Musical Record* 22, no. 260 (August 1, 1892): 175–76.
Pazdírek, Franz, ed. *Universal-Handbuch der Musikliteratur aller Zeiten und Völker.* 16 vols. Vienna: Pazdírek & Co., 1904–10.
Peters, C. F. "Beste und billigste Klassiker-Ausgabe." Unpaginated insert included in *Schwäbischer Merkur* (Stuttgart), no. 284 (December 1, 1869).
Planer, John H. "Sentimentality in the Performance of Absolute Music: Pablo Casals's Performance of Saraband from Johann Sebastian Bach's Suite No. 2 in D Minor for Unaccompanied Cello, S. 1008." *The Musical Quarterly* 73, no. 2 (1989): 212–48.
Podger, Rachel. *J. S. Bach: Cello Suites.* Channel Classics, SA41119, 2019.
Porter, Amy. *In Translation: Selections from J. S. Bach's Cello Suites.* Equilibrium Records, EQ124, 2013.

Bibliography

Pougin, Arthur. "Les Concours du Conservatoire." *Le Ménestrel* 75, no. 29 (July 17, 1909): 227–30.

Poulin, Pamela L., trans. *J. S. Bach's Precepts and Principles for Playing the Thorough-Bass or Accompanying in Four Parts: Leipzig, 1738*. Oxford: Clarendon Press, 1994.

Preece, Thomas, arr. *Selections from the Bach Cello Suites, Arranged for Ukulele*. Self-published, 2015.

Prieto, Carlos. *The Adventures of a Cello*. Translated by Elena C. Murray. Austin: University of Texas Press.

Primrose, William, ed. *Johann Sebastian Bach, Five Suites for Viola*. New York: G. Schirmer, 1978.

Probst, Heinrich Albert, ed. *Six Sonates ou études pour le violoncelle solo composées par J. Sébastien Bach, œuvre posthume*. Leipzig: H. A. Probst, [1825].

Quantz, Johann Joachim. *On Playing the Flute*. Translated by Edward R. Reilly. London: Faber & Faber, 1985.

Rabbath, François. *Bach, Suites pour violoncelle seul à la contrebasse*. Disques du Solstice, SOCD292–93, 2012.

Raff, Joachim, arr. *Sechs Sonaten für Violoncell componirt von Joh. Seb. Bach. Für Pianoforte bearbeitet von Joachim Raff*. Leipzig and Winterthur: J. Reiter-Biedermann, [1870–71].

Rameau, Pierre. *Le maître à danser*. Paris, 1725.

Reichardt, Johann Friedrich. "Einige Anmerkungen zu Forkels Schrift: Ueber Joh. Sebast. Bach." *Berlinische Musikalische Zeitung* 2, no. 51 (1806): 201–2.

Richter, Maik. *Die Hofmusik in Köthen: von den Anfängen (um 1690) bis zum Tod Fürst Leopolds von Anhalt-Köthen*. Saarbrücken: VDM Verlag, 2010.

Romberg, Bernhard. *Méthode de violoncelle*. Paris, [1840].

——. *Violoncell Schule*. Berlin, [1840].

Rose, Stephen. *Musical Authorship from Schütz to Bach*. Cambridge: Cambridge University Press, 2019.

Rothfarb, Lee A. *Ernst Kurth as Theorist and Analyst*. Philadelphia: University of Pennsylvania Press, 2016.

Rousseau, Jean. *Traité de la viole*. Paris, 1687.

Rummel, Martin. *Bach Cello Suites: Kellner Manuscript*. Paladino Music, PMR0004, 2009.

Sainsbury, John, ed. *A Dictionary of Musicians [...]*. 2 vols. London, 1824.

Sanguineti, Alessandro. "Da Spalla or Da Gamba? The Early Cello in Northern Italian Repertoire, 1650–95." *Galpin Society Journal* 69 (April 2016): 99–108.

Schachter, Carl. *The Art of Tonal Analysis: Twelve Lessons in Schenkerian Analysis*. Edited by Joseph N. Straus. Oxford: Oxford University Press, 2015.

Bibliography

"The Prelude from Bach's Suite No. 4 for Violoncello Solo: The Submerged Urlinie." *Current Musicology* 56 (1994): 54–71.

"Rhythm and Linear Analysis: Durational Reduction." In *Unfoldings: Essays in Schenkerian Theory and Analysis*, edited by Joseph N. Straus, 54–78. Oxford: Oxford University Press, 1999.

Schenker, Heinrich. Diary entry dated March 12, 1926. Transcribed by Marko Deislinger. Translated by William Drabkin. www.schenkerdocumentson line.org/documents/diaries/OJ-03–08_1926–03/r0012.html.

"The Sarabande of Bach's Suite No. 3 for Solo Violoncello." Translated by Hedi Siegel. In *The Masterwork in Music: A Yearbook*, vol. 2, edited by William Drabkin, 55–58. Mineola: Dover Publications, 2014.

Schmid, Manfred Hermann. "Das Geschäft mit dem Nachlaß von C. Ph. E. Bach." In *Carl Philipp Emanuel Bach und die europäische Musikkultur des mittleren 18. Jahrhunderts*, edited by Hans-Joachim Marx, 473–528. Göttingen: Vandenhoeck & Ruprecht, 1990.

Schmidt, Annlies. J. S. *Bach: Six Suites pour violoncelle seul*. Forgotten Records, FR118–19, 2009.

Schmidt, Heinrich ("Z"). "Correspondenz: Leipzig." *Neue Zeitschrift für Musik* 61, no. 7 (February 10, 1865): 55–56.

Schulenberg, David. "Composition and Improvisation in the School of J. S. Bach." In *Bach Perspectives 1*, edited by Russell Stinson, 1–42. Lincoln, NE: University of Nebraska Press, 1995.

"Composition as Variation: Inquiries into the Compositional Procedures of the Bach Circle of Composers." *Current Musicology* 33 (1982): 57–87.

The Keyboard Music of J. S. Bach. 2nd ed. New York: Routledge, 2006.

Schulze, Hans-Joachim. "The French Influence in Bach's Instrumental Music." *Early Music* 13, no. 2 (May 1985): 180–84.

"Von Weimar nach Köthen: Risiken und Chancen eines Amtwechsels." *Cöthener Bach-Hefte* 11 (2003): 9–27.

Schulze, Hans-Joachim, ed. *Bach Dokumente. Vol. 3, Dokumente zum Nachwirken Johann Sebastian Bachs, 1685–1750*. Leipzig: Bach-Archiv, 1972.

Schumann, Robert, arr. *Suite III C-dur für Violoncello Solo, BWV 1009 für Violoncello und Klavier*, by J. S. Bach, edited by Joachim Draheim. Wiesbaden: Breitkopf & Härtel, 1985.

Schwanberger, Johann Gottfried. *Verzeichniß der von dem herzogl. Braunschw. Lüneb. Kapellmeister Schwanberg hinterlassenen beträchtlichen Sammlung von Musikalien [. . .]*. Braunschweig, 1806.

Schwemer, Bettina, and Douglas Woodfull-Harris, eds. *6 Suites a Violoncello Solo senza Basso, BWV 1007–1012*, by J. S. Bach. Kassel: Bärenreiter Verlag, 2000.

Sevier, Zay David. "Bach's Solo Violin Sonatas and Partitas: The First Century and a Half" (parts 1 and 2). *BACH* 12, no. 2 (April 1981): 11–19; 12, no. 3 (July 1981): 21–29.

Bibliography

Shihoten, Kevin. "Cellist Performs atop Mt. Fuji." *Playbill*, June 19, 2007. www.playbill.com/article/cellist-performs-atop-mt-fuji.

Siblin, Eric. *The Cello Suites: J. S. Bach, Pablo Casals, and the Search for a Baroque Masterpiece*. New York: Atlantic Monthly Press, 2009.

Sisman, Elaine. "Six of One: The Opus Concept in the Eighteenth Century." In *The Century of Bach and Mozart: Perspectives on Historiography, Composition, Theory, and Performance*, edited by Thomas Forrest Kelly and Sean Gallagher, 79–107. Cambridge, MA: Harvard University Press, 2009.

Smend, Friedrich. *Bach in Köthen*. Translated by John Page. Edited by Stephen Daw. St. Louis: Concordia Publishing House, 1985.

Smith, Mark M. "The Cello Bow Held the Viol-Way: Once Common, but Now Almost Forgotten." *Chelys: The Journal of the Viola da Gamba Society* 24 (1995): 47–60.

———. "A Deceptive Edition of the Bach 'Cello Suites." *BACH* 9, no. 1 (January 1978): 26–29.

Snyder, Robert. *Pablo Casals*. New York: Mannes College of Music, 1955.

Spitta, Philipp. *Johann Sebastian Bach: His Work and Influence on the Music of Germany, 1685–1750*. 3 vols. Translated by Clara Bell and J. A. Fuller Maitland. London, 1899.

Squire, W. H., arr. *Second Violoncello Album*. London: Joseph Williams, 1902.

Stade, Friedrich Wilhelm, arr. *Joh. Seb. Bachs Compositionen für Violoncello solo mit Begleitung des Pianoforte*. Leipzig: Gustav Heinze, [1864].

Stanfield, Milly B. "Silhouettes from Britain." *Violins and Violinists Magazine* 18, no. 3 (May–June 1957): 100–101.

Starker, János. *J. S. Bach: Suites for Solo Cello*. RCA Victor Red Seal, 09026-61436-2, 1997.

Stinson, Russell. *The Bach Manuscripts of Johann Peter Kellner and His Circle: A Case Study in Reception History*. Durham, NC: Duke University Press, 1989.

Stowell, Robin. *The Early Violin and Viola: A Practical Guide*. Cambridge: Cambridge University Press, 2001.

———. "Other Solo Repertory." In *The Cambridge Companion to the Cello*, edited by Robin Stowell, 137–45. Cambridge: Cambridge University Press, 1999.

Stravinsky, Igor, and Robert Craft. *Themes and Episodes*. New York: Alfred A. Knopf, 1966.

Svećenski, Louis. *Johann Sebastian Bach: Six Suites for Violoncello, Adapted, Revised, and Fingered for Viola*. New York: G. Schirmer, 1916.

Szabó, Zoltán. "Precarious Presumptions and the 'Minority Report': Revisiting the Primary Sources of the Bach Cello Suites." *BACH* 45, no. 2 (2014): 1–33.

———. "Problematic Sources, Problematic Transmission: An Outline of the Edition History of the Solo Cello Suites by J. S. Bach." PhD diss., Sydney Conservatorium of Music, 2016.

Bibliography

"Remaining Silhouettes of Lost Bach Manuscripts? Re-evaluating J. P. Kellner's Copy of J. S. Bach's Solo String Compositions." *Understanding Bach* 10 (2015): 71–83.

Talle, Andrew. "Courts." In *The Routledge Research Companion to Johann Sebastian Bach*, ed. Robin A. Leaver, 191–209. New York: Routledge, 2017.

Revised preface to *Six Suites for Violoncello Solo, BWV 1007–1012*, by J. S. Bach, edited by Andrew Talle. Kassel: Bärenreiter Verlag, 2018. 3rd rev. printing, 2022.

"Some Observations on the Sources for Bach's *Violin Soli* and *Cello Suites*." *BACH* 53, no. 1 (2022): 1–44.

"Who Was Anna Magdalena Bach?" *BACH* 51, no. 1 (2020): 139–71.

Taruskin, Richard. "Six Times Six: A Bach Suite Selection." In *The Danger of Music and Other Anti-Utopian Essays*, 66–70. Berkeley: University of California Press, 2009.

Text & Act: Essays on Music and Performance. Oxford: Oxford University Press, 1995.

Tatlow, Ruth. "A Missed Opportunity: Reflections on *Written by Mrs Bach*." *Understanding Bach* 10 (March 2015): 141–57.

Tatton, Thomas. "Bach Violoncello Suites Arranged for Viola: Available Editions Annotated." *Journal of the American Viola Society* 27 (Summer 2011): 5–27.

Tauber, Gottfried. *Rechtschaffener Tanzmeister, oder gründliche Erklärung der frantzösischen Tantz-Künst*. 3 vols. Leipzig, 1717.

Taubman, Howard. "Musicians' Guild Ends Fine Season." *The New York Times*, March 8, 1949: 31.

Tinbergen, B. E. "The 'Cello' in the Low Countries: The Instrument and Its Practical Use in the 17th and 18th Centuries." PhD diss., Leiden University, 2018.

Tingler, Nathan David. "Bach and the Marimba: Bridging the Gap to Non-Percussionists." DMA diss., University of Georgia, 2020.

Tobel, Rudolf von. *Pablo Casals*. 2nd ed. Zurich: Rotapfel-Verlag, 1945.

Tomita, Yo. "Anna Magdalena as Bach's Copyist." *Understanding Bach* 2 (2007): 59–76.

Traeg, Johann. *Verzeichniß alter und neuer sowohl geschriebener als gestochener Musikalien*. Vienna, 1799.

Treitler, Leo, ed. *Strunk's Source Readings in Music History*. Rev. ed. New York: W. W. Norton, 1998.

Van der Straeten, E., and Lynda MacGregor. "Dotzauer, (Justus Johann) Friedrich." In *Grove Music Online*, edited by Deane Root. Published January 20, 2001.

Vanscheeuwijck, Marc. "The Baroque Cello and Its Performance." *Performance Practice Review* 9, no. 1 (Spring 1996): 78–96.

Bibliography

"Recent Re-evaluations of the Baroque Cello and What They Might Mean for Performing the Music of J. S. Bach." *Early Music* 48, no. 2 (May 2010): 181–92.

Venturini, Adriana. "The Dresden School of Violoncello in the Nineteenth Century." MA thesis, University of Central Florida, 2009.

Viole, Rudolph. "Aus Berlin." *Neue Zeitschrift für Musik* 48, no. 14 (April 2, 1858): 151–52.

Wadsworth, Kate Bennett. "'Precisely Marked in the Tradition of the Composer': The Performing Editions of Friedrich Grützmacher." PhD diss., University of Leeds, 2017.

Walther, Johann Gottfried. *Musicalisches Lexikon*. Leipzig, 1732.

——. *Praecepta der musicalischen Composition*. Edited by Peter Benary. Leipzig: Breitkopf & Härtel, 1955.

Wangenheim, Andreas von. *J. S. Bach: Six Suites for Violoncello Solo (Transcription for Guitar)*. Arte Nova Classics, ANO675220, 1999.

Weilerstein, Alisa. *Bach*. Pentatone, PTC5186751, 2020.

Whitehouse, William. *Recollections of a Violoncellist*. London: The Strad Office, 1930.

Williams, Amédée Daryl. *Lillian Fuchs, First Lady of the Viola*. 2nd rev. ed. Lincoln, NE: iUniverse Inc., 2004.

Wilson, Miranda. *The Well-Tempered Cello: Life with Bach Cello Suites*. Austin: Fairhaven Press, 2022.

Wise, Brian. "Why Are Cellists So Often Involved in Political Causes?" *Strings Magazine* 37, no. 315 (November–December 2023): 40–44.

Wissick, Brent. "The Cello Music of Antonio Bononcini: Violone, Violoncello da Spalla, and the Cello 'Schools' of Bologna and Rome." *Journal of Seventeenth-Century Music* 12, no. 2 (2006). www.sscm-jscm.org/v12/no1/wissick.html.

Wolf, Hugo. *The Music Criticism of Hugo Wolf*. Translated and edited by Henry Pleasants. New York: Holmes & Meier, 1978.

Wolff, Christoph. *Bach's Musical Universe: The Composer and His Work*. New York: W. W. Norton, 2020.

——. *Johann Sebastian Bach: The Learned Musician*. Updated ed. New York: W. W. Norton, 2013.

Wong, Max H. Y. "Arrangements as a Creative Tool towards the Performance of J. S. Bach's Six Sonatas and Partitas for Solo Violin, BWV 1001–1006." PhD diss., Royal College of Music, 2023.

Yamashita Kazuhito. *J. S. Bach: The Complete Suites for Solo Cello, Guitar Version*. Crown Classics, CRCC8003–4, 1993.

Yapp, Francis. "*Les Prétentions du Violoncelle*: The Cello as a Solo Instrument in France in the Pre-Duport Era (1700–1760)." PhD diss., University of Canterbury, 2012.

Yearsley, David. *Sex, Death, and Minuets: Anna Magdalena and Her Musical Notebooks*. Chicago: University of Chicago Press, 2019.

Bibliography

Youngerman, Irit. "J. S. Bach's Suite in C Major for Violoncello Solo: An Analysis through Application of a Historical Approach." MM thesis, University of Cincinnati, 2002.

Zimmermann, Agnes, arr. *Bourrée in C by J. S. Bach*. London, [1868].

Bourrée in E♭ by J. S. Bach. London, [1868].

Gavotte in G by J. S. Bach. London, [1868].

INDEX

Abel, Christian Ferdinand, 5–7, 28
Agricola, Johann Friedrich, 8, 82, 84
Alexanian, Diran, 122, 131
Altnikol, Johann Christoph, 81–82

Bach, Anna Magdalena, 1, 11, 63–69,
    72–76, 84, 100, 120, 122, 132
Bach, C. P. E.
  Cello Suites manuscript owned by, 8,
    71–72, 74–75, 81–85
  on his father's Cello Suites and Violin
    Solos, 8–9, 14, 69
  on improvising preludes, 47–49
  at the Prussian court, 26–27, 70–71
Bach, J. S., Cello Suites
  Cello Suite No. 1 (BWV1007)
    analysis and style of, 34, 37–39,
      43–44, 46, 48–49
    historical editions of, 86, 88, 96–98,
      100–101, 105
    modernist adaptation of, 137
    in multimedia, 132, 137–138, 141–142
    and Pablo Casals, 120
    performances of, 90–93, 103
  Cello Suite No. 2 (BWV1008)
    analysis and style of, 34, 45–46,
      128–129
    historical editions of, 88, 94, 122
    and Pablo Casals, 115, 120–122
    performances of, 102, 126
    variants in manuscripts sources of, 73
  Cello Suite No. 3 (BWV1009)
    analysis and style of, 16, 34–35,
      37–38, 39–40, 44–45, 129–130
    arrangements and transcriptions of,
      92, 96
    historical editions of, 98
    and Pablo Casals, 115, 120, 129–130
    performances of, 102, 124–125
    tempo of Prelude, 75–76, 88

Cello Suite No. 4 (BWV1010)
  analysis and style of, 41, 45–46, 49–58
  dynamics in manuscript sources of, 75
  historical editions of, 94
  key of, 14, 47
  performances of, 93, 106
  speculative Christian interpretation of
    Prelude, 52–54
Cello Suite No. 5 (BWV1011).
    See also scordatura
  analysis and style of, 16, 34, 36–38,
    41–42, 46–47, 48
  historical editions of, 85–86, 94–95,
    96–98, 101
  lute transcription of, 75–76
  manuscript sources of, 65, 69–70
  in multimedia, 117, 142
  and Pablo Casals, 123–124
  performances of, 94–95, 133
Cello Suite No. 6 (BWV1012).
    See also cello, five-string
  analysis of, 6, 34, 37, 40, 128–129
  brilliant style of, 14, 41, 46
  historical editions of, 86–89, 96, 98, 101
  manuscript sources of, 70, 75
  performances of, 103, 127, 133–134
  rustic style of Gavotte II ("la Musette"),
    40, 89, 103, 105–106
in general
  accompaniment (piano or organ),
    90–94, 100, 106
  as a collection, 7–14, 131
  concerts of complete cycle, 133–134
  during the COVID-19 pandemic, 117,
    142–143
  dynamics in, 57, 74–76, 88, 101, 105,
    123, 130–131
  as études or student/training
    repertoire, 9, 85–87, 89–91,
    94–96, 101–102, 119–120, 141

Index

in film and television, 139–142
French reception of, 96, 102–103
as humanitarian advocacy, 116–117
implied polyphony in, 16, 43–45, 82–83, 122, 128–131
imprecise references as "sonatas" (instead of "suites"), 8, 68–69, 83–84, 86, 88, 92, 96
as inspiration for new compositions, 137
as inspiration for pop music, 137–138
in literature, nonfiction, and theater, 139
manuscript sources of, 8, 10–11, 57, 62–77, 100–101, 120, 131–132
in modern dance and ballet, 139
negative appraisals of, 90–91, 99, 104
performances on mountains, 141
positive appraisals of, 8–9, 86–87, 92, 95, 117–119, 132
preludes, 47–49
recordings of, 72, 106, 115–116, 119–127, 131–132, 136–141, 142–143
on social media, 136, 141–143
in transcriptions for other instruments, 75–76, 92–93, 94–96, 136–139
unity within each suite, 42–47
in visual art, 138–139
Bach, J. S., other works
Brandenburg Concertos (BWV1046–51), 2, 7, 11
Christ lag in Todesbanden (BWV4), 54
Clavier-Übung I (BWV825–30), 7, 12, 36
English Suites (BWV806–11), 12, 37, 40
French Ouverture (BWV831), 75
French Suites (BWV812–17), 2, 41–43, 75
Fugue in G Minor for Violin and Continuo (BWV1026), 10
Lute Suite No. 5 in G Minor (BWV995), 75–76
Orchestral Suite No. 3 in D Major (BWV1068), 102
Partita for Solo Flute (BWV1013), 36
Sonatas and Partitas for Solo Violin (BWV1001–6), 1, 7–16, 27–28, 34–36, 57, 74, 80–85, 90–92, 94–95, 115, 128, 143

Sonatas for Viola da Gamba and Harpsichord (BWV1027–29), 5
St. Matthew Passion (BWV244), 53
Well-Tempered Clavier (BWV846–93), 2, 7, 33, 48, 102, 116
Bach-Gesellschaft, 99–101
Bach in the Subways, 134
Badiarov, Dmitry, 136
Baroque dances. *See* suite (as instrumental genre); tempo
Becker, Hugo, 101, 104–106, 115, 120, 130
Biber, Heinrich Ignaz Franz, 15, 53
Bloch, Ernest, 137
Block, Mike, 137
Boden, Ruth, 141
Bosmans, Henri, 136
bowing
bariolage, 48
chord rolling, 91, 96, 131, 135
flying staccato, 98
portato, 105
underhand bow hold, 26–27, 77, 136
Britten, Benjamin, 137
Brunello, Mario, 141
Bülow, Hans von, 102
Bylsma, Anner, 72–73, 136

Cabisius, Julius, 92
Casals, Pablo, 80–81, 86, 101, 103, 106, 115–132
Cassadó, Gaspar, 137
Castro, Max Oróbio de, 133–134
cello, five-string. *See also* Bach, J. S.: Cello Suite No. 6 (BWV1012)
indications in manuscripts and editions, 69–70, 87
modern revival of, 135–136
viola pomposa and violoncello piccolo, 11
Cöthen, 1–2, 4–7, 10–11, 12–15, *See also* Leopold, Prince of Anhalt-Cöthen

dances, Baroque. *See* suite (as instrumental genre); tempo
David, Ferdinand, 80, 94–95, 96
DeCesare, Nina, 143
Delsart, Jules, 103

Index

Dörffel, Alfred, 99–101
Dotzauer, Justus Johann Friedrich, 88–90, 92, 96, 105

Eisenberg, Maurice, 120

Fischer, Norman, 134
five-string cello. *See* cello, five-string
Forkel, Johann Nikolaus, 8–9, 14, 34, 82–84
Foss, Lukas, 137
Freed, David, 134
French manners in German courts, 2–7
French titles for suite movements, 12, 34–35, 38–39
Fuchs, Lillian, 126–127

Gabrielli, Domenico, 7
Gál, Hans, 137
Gerber, Ernst Ludwig, 84
Grädener, Carl, 92, 93, 100
Graul, Markus Heinrich, 26
Greenhouse, Bernard, 122
Gregson, Peter, 137, 141
Grützmacher, Friedrich, 94, 96–99, 101, 103–106, 119

Haimovitz, Matt, 72
Harndorff, Édouard-André, 103
Harnoncourt, Nikolaus, 136
Harrison, Beatrice, 106, 123
Hartshorne, Richard, 136
Hausmann, Robert, 101, 104–106, 115
hemiola, 36–37, 57
Henderson, Dale, 134
historical performance, 134–136
Honegger, Henri, 133
Hulshoff, Gerrit, 130–132

Joachim, Joseph, 80, 94, 95, 101–102
Johansen, Dane, 141

Karachevtsev, Denys, 117
Kelley, Edgar Stillman, 90–91, 92
Kellner, Johann Peter, 65–70, 72–76, 82–83, 88
Kirnberger, Johann Philipp, 33, 35, 83–84

Klengel, Julius, 91, 101, 106, 120, 123, 124, 133
Kuijken, Sigiswald, 136
Kurth, Ernst, 128–129, 131

Leisinger, Ulrich, 71–72, 74
Leopold, Prince of Anhalt-Cöthen, 1–3, 4–5, 6–7, 10
Linike, Christian Bernhard, 5, 26, 81
Loevensohn, Marix, 103
Lübeck, Louis, 104
Lully, Jean-Baptiste, 3, 4

Ma, Yo-Yo, 117, 132, 134–135, 138
Machy, Sieur de, 5–6
MacLaine, Julia, 137
Maisky, Mischa, 134
Mattheson, Johann, 18–19, 33–41
Meyer, Edgar, 136
Mozart, Leopold, 20, 73
Müller, Wilhelm, 102

Neikrug, George, 134
Niedt, Friedrich Erhard, 43, 50
Norblin, Louis-Pierre, 85–89, 92, 100

Paris Conservatoire, 87, 102, 103
Piatti, Alfredo, 91, 93–94, 101
Pisendel, Johann Georg, 15–16
Poëncet, Henry-Marie-Joseph, 102
Popper, David, 93
portamento, 88–89, 98, 105–106, 123
Prieto, Carlos, 134
Primrose, William, 127
Probst, Heinrich Albert, 88

Quantz, Johann Joachim, 20, 27, 73
Queyras, Jean-Guihen, 139

Rabbath, François, 136
Rameau, Pierre, 3
Reger, Max, 137
Reichardt, Johann Friedrich, 83
Reimers, Christian, 92
Rostropovich, Mstislav, 117–118, 134
Rousseau, Jean, 5–6
Royal Academy of Music, 102
Rummel, Martin, 73

Index

Schenker, Heinrich, 129–130
Schetky, Johann Georg Christoph, 26
Schmidt-de Neveu, Annlies, 136
Schneider, Mischa, 130
Schober, Johann Nikolaus, 70–71, 72, 74
Schumann, Robert, 90–94, 98
Schwanberger, Georg Heinrich Ludwig, 11, 64, 84
scordatura, 7, 14, 46, 69–70, 85–86, 101, 131
Squire, William Henry, 105–106
Stade, Friedrich Wilhelm, 92–93, 105–106
Starker, János, 132
Suggia, Guilhermina, 124–125
suite (as instrumental genre), 33–49
Šulić, Luka, 141
Sutter, Wendy, 139
Suzuki Shin'ichi, 95
Svećenski, Louis, 127
Swert, Jules de, 94

Talle, Andrew, 62, 64, 65, 67–77, 81–82
Telemann, Georg Philipp, 15
tempo
  and Baroque dances, 37, 39, 41, 57
  in Cello Suites editions, 81, 88–89, 96, 106, 115
  in Cello Suites manuscripts, 74–76, 88–89
  in Cello Suites recordings, 106, 115, 123
Traeg, Johann, 71, 83–84

Vandini, Antonio, 26
vibrato, 102, 105, 106, 123
viol (viola da gamba), 1, 3, 5–7, 136
viola da spalla, 1, 16–28, 77, 136
violoncello piccolo. *See under* cello, five-string

Walther, Johann Gottfried, 19–22, 33–40, 43
Weilerstein, Alisa, 137, 142–143
Westhoff, Johann Paul von, 15
Whitehouse, William, 93–94, 102, 106
Wiesel, Uzi, 134
Wohlers, Heinrich, 103
Wolf, Hugo, 104
Wolff, Christian, 137
Wolff, Christoph, 7, 10, 15, 27

Yellin, Thelma, 134

For EU product safety concerns, contact us at Calle de José Abascal, 56–1°, 28003 Madrid, Spain or eugpsr@cambridge.org.

www.ingramcontent.com/pod-product-compliance
Lightning Source LLC
LaVergne TN
LVHW020346260326
834688LV00045B/1564